MW01043062

"The guy who got so many of us hooked on Formula 1 today has turned his attention to getting us hooked on everything that got us to this point. *Grand Prix* introduced me to so many stories I never knew and so many races I want to go back and watch."

—JANNIK SINNER, Grand Slam tennis champion

"There's nothing like the buzz of a Grand Prix and nothing like the passion of its incredible fans. Will Buxton has played a huge role in telling the modern story of F1 to us all, but here he takes us on a journey to the past. It's the ultimate guide to the greatest sport."

—MARTIN GARRIX, DJ

"I'm a huge believer that sport is for everyone. No one should ever feel left out just because they've only just got into it. Will Buxton is knowledgeable and authoritative but always welcoming of new people who might fall in love with his favorite sport. This book is perfect for newcomers who want to take their F1 obsession to the next level and for the diehards."

—GREG JAMES, broadcaster and author

"Will Buxton brings his boyish enthusiasm and depth of knowledge together in this fascinating, exciting, and completely approachable book on Formula 1. It's a must for all Formula 1 fans."

—TOM KERRIDGE, chef patron

"Having been lucky enough to share F1 pitlanes and paddocks of the world with Will Buxton, I know how much he loves the sport and the history that goes with it. This is an invaluable book for newcomers and established fans of the greatest sport on the planet. Will, with his love of the sport, is the perfect guy to guide you through it."

—JAKE HUMPHREY, broadcaster

GRAND PRIX

AN ILLUSTRATED HISTORY OF FORMULA 1

GRAND PRIX

WILL BUXTON

ILLUSTRATIONS BY DAVI AUGUSTO
FOREWORD BY STEFANO DOMENICALI

TEN SPEED PRESS

California | New York

CONTENTS

FOREWORD

I was born in the town of Imola. It is quite a small and usually quiet town in the north of Italy. But at its heart, there is a racetrack. One of the best in the world. My earliest memories are of the sound of racing cars. Playing games at school pretending to be our racing heroes. Trying to catch a glimpse of the cars over the wall of the track, and through the trees.

You see, racing is in my blood. For almost every Italian, it is something engrained in us from birth, thanks in no small part to the specter of Ferrari, the most famous and successful team in the history of the greatest motor racing championship in the world, Formula 1.

My only dream was to work for Ferrari. And with immense gratitude, I began my career there shortly after graduating from university. I spent many years at Maranello, and to my delight was appointed not only to work for the Formula 1 racing team, Scuderia Ferrari, but to be its Team Principal.

Today, I am the CEO of Formula 1 itself. It is something I still find difficult to believe. That a boy from Imola could one day play such a role in developing and growing the sport I have loved my entire life. It is the greatest honor.

I say this to tell you what motorsport, and more importantly Formula 1, means to me.

I take huge pride in seeing how much the sport has grown in recent years. How truly internationally popular it has become. While it has always been a global sport, loved around the world, it has never received the attention and the fanaticism with which it is greeted today. And I am aware that while for many of us racing is a part of our DNA, to some this world of Formula 1 is brand new.

I'm sure most of you know Will from his work on *Formula 1: Drive to Survive* and for us on F1 TV. I first met him twenty years ago when he was just starting out as a young journalist. He was very… how to say… passionate? Quite intense. I'm happy to report he hasn't changed much in all that time. That love of Formula 1 has never wavered. But his passion for this sport is aligned to a deep knowledge and love for the history of Formula 1. Over the years he has become a fantastic storyteller, allowing fans old and new a unique perspective into the sport.

His idea for this book, to create an accessible guide to the drivers and teams at the heart of the history of our sport, is something special. I hope you enjoy reading about all of those who went before, and who created what we know today as Formula 1. As we look back over more than seventy years and more than one thousand races, I'm filled with excitement for the opportunity of all that stands ahead.

—STEFANO DOMENICALI
President and CEO of Formula 1

WHAT IS FORMULA 1?

For more than seventy years, Formula 1 has been the pinnacle of global motorsport, the ultimate test of machine and humankind. With over twenty races on some of the most challenging circuits ever built, in some of the most glamorous locations around the world, competing at this level is seen as the zenith of a racing driver's career. To win in this sport is an almost impossibly difficult task. To tally enough success to be crowned champion is therefore to have your name placed alongside the very greatest this sport has ever known.

Formula 1 is high-speed, high-stakes racing. Drivers do battle at over 200 mph, just millimeters apart, moments from disaster, combining incredible skill with awe-inspiring bravery in a singular quest to prove that they are the very best on their day and in their game. Their journey to the pinnacle of racing begins in childhood, their talent developed from go-karts, through junior open wheel careers, to the very top of the sport. As their competitive instincts sharpen, their desire and hunger to win against all odds and against all challengers becomes an intrinsic part of their personalities. Over time, through a combination of ability, experience, defeat, victory, perseverance, and prowess, their goal is to become the ultimate driver.

At their command are the fastest and most advanced open wheel racing cars of all time. These rocket ships on wheels are comprised of thousands of unique parts, designed and manufactured specifically for racing by a team of thousands of people, whose own expertise is as essential to winning a race as is the craft of the racer behind the wheel. Hundreds of millions of dollars are spent in the pursuit of glory. Decisions during a race are made in the blink of an eye, from the driver in the heat of battle to the strategist calling the race-winning shots and the pit crew servicing the cars and sending them on their way in mere seconds. Those who succeed know that on their day, and in their moment, there was no car as fast, no team as regimented, no driver as good.

The challenge, always, is to win. And to keep winning. And for those who don't, to fight, to catch, to overhaul, and to then begin their own era of domination by taking the two biggest prizes in motorsport: the Formula 1 Drivers' World Championship and the Formula 1 Constructors' World Championship. But what does it take to become the best? Who are the greatest of all time? How has this sport become the global phenomenon that it is, and what does its future hold?

In this book, you will discover all that Formula 1 is today and all that went before, from the story of how this incredible championship has evolved to the teams who made the greatest cars of their generation. On this decade-by-decade journey through the history of the sport, you'll be introduced to every champion the sport has crowned. And while I'd love to write about every driver this sport has known, time and space sadly won't permit such a luxury. Instead, and for every decade, you'll also read about one unique racer who I believe had all the skill but never won the championship, along with a handful of notable drivers of each generation. And we'll take a step back in time to relive some of the greatest races the sport has ever seen.

This is where technical genius meets sporting excellence. This is where dreamers become heroes and where icons are forged in the white heat of pure competition.

This is the pinnacle of motor racing. This is Formula 1.

ABU DHABI (1)
Yas Marina

ARGENTINA (1)
Buenos Aires

AUSTRALIA (2)
Adelaide
Melbourne

AUSTRIA (2)
Spielberg
Zeltweg

AZERBAIJAN (1)
Baku

BAHRAIN (1)
Sakhir

BELGIUM (3)
Nivelles
Spa
Zolder

BRAZIL (2)
Rio
São Paulo

CANADA (3)
Mont-Tremblant
Montreal
Mosport

CHINA (1)
Shanghai

FRANCE (7)
Clermont-Ferrand
Dijon
Le Castellet
Le Mans
Magny-Cours
Reims
Rouen

GERMANY (3)
Berlin
Hockenheim
Nürburgring

GREAT BRITAIN (4)
Aintree
Brands Hatch
Donington
Silverstone

HUNGARY (1)
Budapest

INDIA (1)
Greater Noida

ITALY (4)
Imola
Monza
Mugello
Pescara

JAPAN (3)
Aida
Fuji
Suzuka

SOUTH KOREA (1)
Mokpo

MALAYSIA (1)
Kuala Lumpur

MEXICO (1)
Mexico City

WHERE DOES FORMULA 1 RACE?

In the more than seventy years of Formula 1, the sport has raced all around the world. Today, the calendar features more than twenty races in twenty different nations. Yet some circuits have remained on the schedule from the very first season in 1950, which comprised just seven races. Let's take a look at everywhere F1 has raced ... so far!

● Active Circuit ● Inactive Circuit

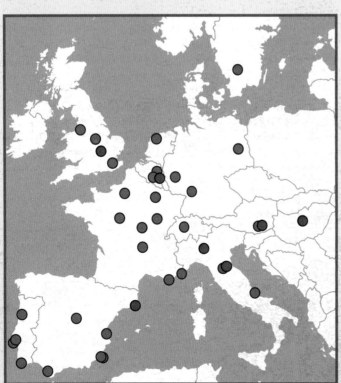

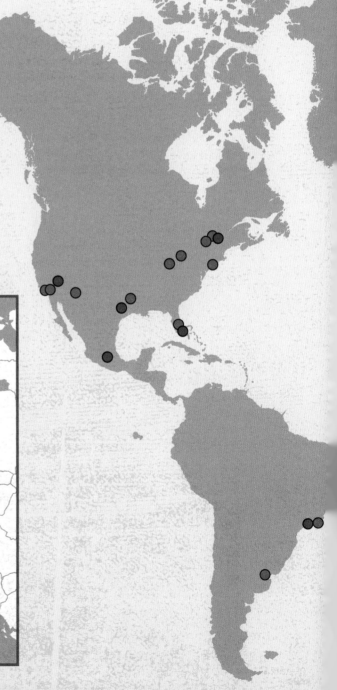

MONACO (1)
Monte Carlo

MOROCCO (1)
Casablanca

NETHERLANDS (1)
Zandvoort

PORTUGAL (4)
Estoril
Lisbon
Portimão
Porto

QATAR (1)
Losail

RUSSIA (1)
Sochi

SAUDI ARABIA (1)
Jeddah

SINGAPORE (1)
Singapore

SOUTH AFRICA (2)
East London
Johannesburg

SPAIN (6)
Barcelona
Jarama
Jerez
Montjuïc
Pedralbes
Valencia

SWEDEN (1)
Anderstorp

SWITZERLAND (1)
Bern

TURKEY (1)
Istanbul

USA (11)
Austin
Dallas
Detroit
Glen Watkins
Indianapolis
Las Vegas
Long Beach
Miami
Phoenix
Riverside
Sebring

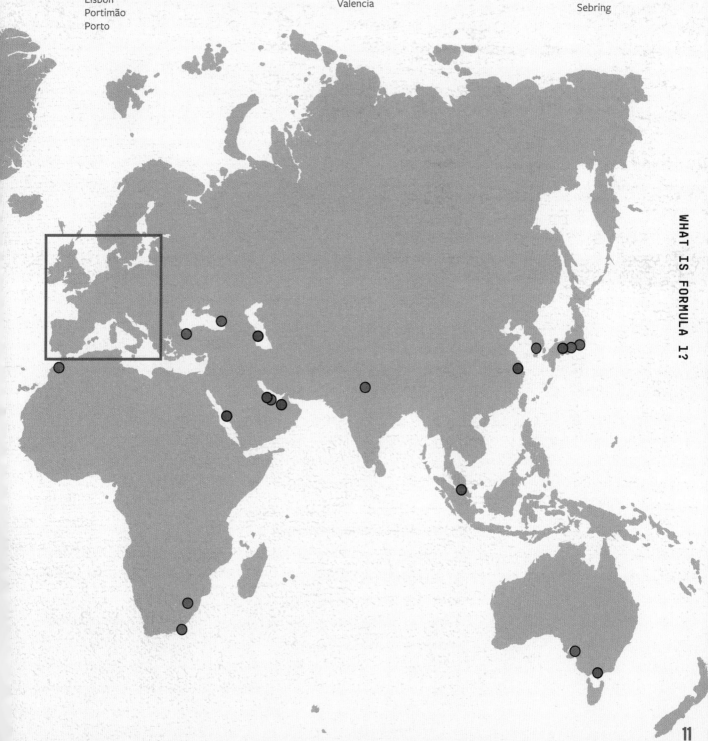

ICONIC FORMULA 1 TRACKS

There have been more Grand Prix venues than years the championship has existed. But while every circuit has played a unique role in the history of Formula 1, some hold a special status as iconic tracks, whose twists and turns are woven into the very fabric of the sport.

MONACO

Seen by many as the ultimate street track and one of the most glamorous races in the world, framed on one side by mountains and on the other by the crystal azure of the Mediterranean Sea, Monaco has been holding Grands Prix on the roads of Monte Carlo since 1929. If anyone was to propose the Monaco Grand Prix as a new race today, they would be laughed out of the room—the speeds are too vast, the track is too small, and the notion of closing down the major road network of a small principality to hold a motor race would be deemed borderline lunacy. Yet it remains on the calendar as the gleaming jewel in Formula 1's crown. There is no challenge as great, no track as demanding or as punishing. Funneled in between metal barriers, the 3.3 km (2-mile) circuit features nineteen corners and is taken in around a minute and ten seconds at full qualifying speed. Drivers describe racing there as being almost hypnotic and trance-like, as their senses become attuned to tackling the narrow streets. One small lapse in focus, one tiny mistake, and it's race over. There are no second chances. Nowhere demands greater skill. No win means as much. Thus has it ever been, and thus will it always remain.

NOW

SUZUKA

In the late 1950s, Soichiro Honda made the decision to build a permanent racetrack near his new automotive factory in Suzuka, Japan. Two years after the factory opened its doors in 1960, his racetrack became reality. It took another twenty-five years until Suzuka welcomed Formula 1, but once it did, it became the favored home of the Japanese Grand Prix and one of the most revered tracks on the calendar. Suzuka is unique in Formula 1 in that it is the only circuit on the schedule designed around a figure-eight layout. Its combination of fast, sweeping changes in direction, off-camber corners, and undulation make it a tremendous challenge for car and driver alike. Each of its corners poses a distinct challenge, from the Degner double-right complex to the long Spoon left-hander and the notoriously fast 130R. Throw the curveball of rain into the mix, as so often happens, and the combination makes for an epic spectacle. There are few circuits as universally loved by Formula 1 drivers as Suzuka, since to master its complex challenges remains a true barometer of the racer behind the wheel.

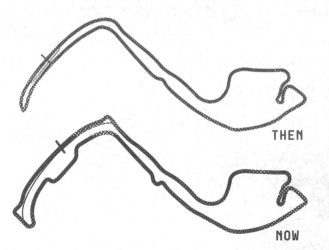

THEN

NOW

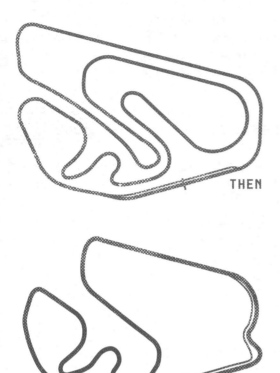

THEN

NOW

INTERLAGOS

Built in 1940, Interlagos has hosted the Brazilian Grand Prix at various times through the 1970s and 1980s, and from 1990 to the present day. In its original form, it was almost 8 km in length, starting with two flat-out banked left-hand corners where today the grandstands sit. From there it looped around and back up to the Curva do Sol, which is still raced today in the opposite direction, before swinging back to the final half of the circuit that we know in the modern era. It took on its current design in 1990 and has remained relatively unchanged ever since, providing the backdrop to a number of classic races that have defined Grand Prix seasons and championship successes. The circuit is famed for its huge elevation changes—most notably the steep climb out of Junção, which brings the drivers back to the start line—and for a flowing nature that naturally lends itself to close racing and thrilling action. It has long been a driver favorite, and the atmosphere at the track is electrifying, thanks to the deep passion for the sport exhibited by the fans who flood the circuit and pack out its grandstands.

INDIANAPOLIS

One of the most famous circuits in the world, the Indianapolis Motor Speedway has existed in two distinct forms in its Formula 1 history. For the first decade of the world championship, the Indy 500 counted as a round of the Formula 1 World Championship, despite the fact that Formula 1 cars have never competed in the race. The unique two-hundred-lap, five-hundred-mile contest around the oval Super Speedway has therefore forever created an anomaly for statisticians. While the winner of the Indy 500 between 1950 and 1960 can't be considered a Grand Prix winner, as the race wasn't run to F1 regulations, they were nevertheless still a winner of a round of the Formula 1 World Championship. The Indy 500 stopped being counted after 1960, but Formula 1 returned to Indy as the home of the US Grand Prix from 2000 to 2007 on a specially designed infield circuit that ran the wrong way around a third of the famous oval, and which is today used by IndyCar for the Indy Grand Prix, the curtain raiser to the month of May festivities and racing action around the Indy 500.

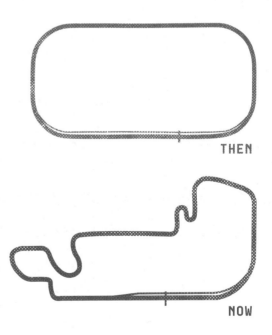

THEN

NOW

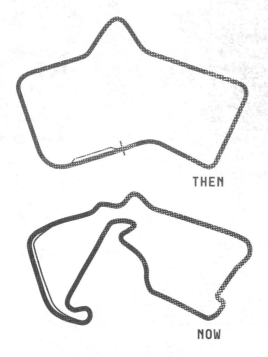

THEN

NOW

SILVERSTONE

The very first world championship race was held in 1950 on the perimeter road of a Second World War airfield, in the heart of the United Kingdom. Silverstone was originally a fast, flowing track consisting of just eight corners, and it proved to be a favorite among drivers. It has remained on the Formula 1 calendar for much of the sport's history, receiving numerous redesigns over its life. The greatest redesign came in the early 1990s when the now-infamous Maggots and Becketts corners were introduced, a staggeringly tricky high-speed sequence of alternating left-right corners over a blind crest. The tweaks continued until a major revamp in 2010 saw the repositioning of the pitlane and start line, and a brand-new infield sequence of corners was added to take the track length up from its original 4.6 km to 5.8 km (2.9 to 3.6 miles). Still revered as one of the drivers' favorites, Silverstone today combines a number of places to attempt overtaking, with long, fast, flowing stretches punctuated by slower switchbacks. And no matter if the British weather decides to deliver bright summer sunshine or deluge the circuit with rain, fierce competition is always a hallmark of the circuit and its races. That, combined with a committed fan base that has turned out in droves since the very first Grand Prix, makes it one of the classic venues for Formula 1.

NÜRBURGRING

Few racing circuits on Earth have created the same level of mystique and fear as the Nürburgring. Originally built in 1927, the full circuit, known as the Gesamtstrecke, consisted of over 187 corners over 28 km (17.4 miles) of winding mayhem through the forests of the Eifel mountains in Germany. When it was first used for Formula 1 in 1951, the circuit had been shortened into the now-legendary Nordschleife, which at a more modest 22 km (13.7 miles) consisted of just 160 corners. It was notoriously treacherous and almost impossible to keep safe—so much so it became known as the "Green Hell." Even the introduction of barriers along its entire length and circuit modifications to eliminate its famous jumps couldn't negate the dangers. It was simply so vast that if anyone crashed, getting to their aid took too long. It was eventually removed from the world championship in the late 1970s. Then, in the 1980s, a new Grand Prix circuit was built to the south of the infamous northern loop. The GP-Strecke was a far more sedate 4.5 km (2.8 miles) and more in keeping with modern trends, while its undulation maintained at least a small element of what had existed before. In total, twenty-two races were held on the Nordschleife and nineteen on the GP-Strecke, but as the calendar expanded out of Europe, the track's finances crumbled and it fell off the full-time schedule in the 2010s. But the aura of the track, and the fearsome challenge of its original layout, marks its place as one of the most awe-inspiring circuits at which Formula 1 has ever raced.

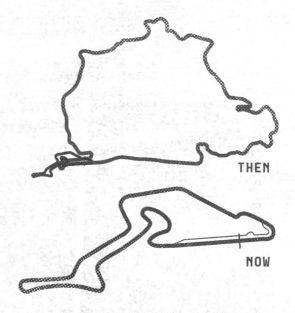

THEN

NOW

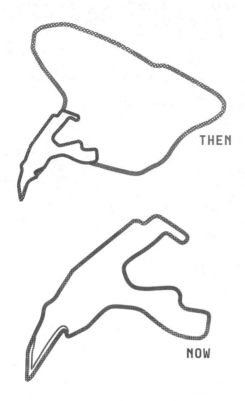

THEN

NOW

SPA-FRANCORCHAMPS

Back in 1920, two friends felt that the country roads around the Belgian towns of Francorchamps, Malmedy, and Stavelot were so much fun to drive that they plotted a route and created a racetrack. Thus, Spa-Francorchamps was born. Just short of 15 km (9.3 miles), it was a mighty challenge, involving massive elevation changes and long blasts through the countryside. During the Second World War, the area became synonymous with the Battle of the Bulge, Germany's last major aggression and the single largest battle fought by the United States in the conflict. When Grand Prix racing began again after the war, the track had been shortened to 14 km (8.7 miles) and became recognized as one of the most difficult on the new world championship calendar. The fearsome Masta Kink was viewed as one of the toughest corners in the world. Yet so perilous did the track become as speeds increased that the race was boycotted in 1969. Changes made a decade later shortened the track to its current 7 km (4.3-mile) configuration. Rather than disappear into the countryside, the track now pulled right at Malmedy, wound its way down the hillside, and picked back up to the old circuit at the bottom of the hill for the rise back to the start line. It remains one of the longest tracks in Formula 1 and one of its purest challenges.

MONZA

The Royal Park of Monza, close to Italy's fashion capital Milan, has played host to a Grand Prix for every season of the world championship except for 1980. Home to Ferrari's loyal fans, the Tifosi, it has an atmosphere unmatched at almost any other Grand Prix venue, as the Italian faithful climb houses and trees within the circuit confines to get the best view of the action. Built in 1922, the original track was 10 km (6.2 miles) in length, composed of a 5.5 km (3.4-mile) road circuit and a 4.5 km (2.8-mile) oval. The road track has remained nearly unchanged ever since, its layout consisting of almost exclusively right-hand corners, save for the left-handers that pull the drivers down onto the back straight. The full 10 km (6.2-mile) track was only used on a few occasions in the 1960s for Grand Prix racing, as drivers would complete the road track before hurtling onto the oval and back again onto the road track, utilizing a split start/finish straight. In 1971 the road track was run for the last time in its pure form as a high-speed challenge. From then on, multiple chicanes were added to bring speeds down on its mighty straights. Yet it remains one of the quickest tracks on the calendar, and the race's complete time is almost always the shortest due to the colossal speeds employed. Loved by all, there is a magic to Monza that is almost impossible to encapsulate, the stories of its history carried as a whisper on the wind through the trees that have stood for centuries and witnessed every champion driver the sport has ever known.

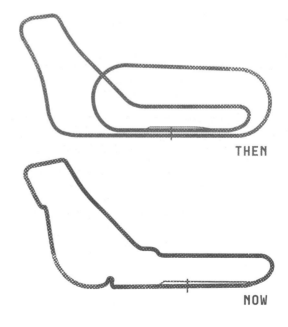

THEN

NOW

FORMULA 1 BASICS

Being a great driver isn't enough to succeed in Formula 1. If you want to win races and championships, you need to race for the best team and drive the best car. Despite drivers being seen as the heroes, Formula 1 is a team sport, and today F1 comprises ten teams, which are also known as "constructors." By the rules, each team must design and manufacture their own unique car, of which two must be entered at every race of the world championship. While in years gone by teams were allocated race numbers as entrants, today drivers choose their own personal race numbers, with the champion able to switch to running number "1."

Every year a maximum of twenty-four races take place around the world, with every team entering two drivers. Their finishing positions are rewarded with points scored equally by the driver and their team. At the end of the season, the driver who scores the most points is named Drivers' World Champion, and the team whose drivers have brought in the most points is named Constructors' World Champion. It is a complicated specialty of Formula 1 that team-mates race together to bring success to their teams, and yet are also battling to beat each other and prove that they are the best and win their own individual title.

Ferrari is the oldest and most successful team in the sport. They're the only team to have taken part in every season in F1 history, and they top the all-time championship list with sixteen Constructors' titles. Williams has nine Constructors' Championships, with McLaren and Mercedes tied with eight. Ferrari has taken a driver to the world championship fifteen times, with McLaren achieving the feat twelve times and Mercedes nine. Of those drivers, Sir Lewis Hamilton and Michael Schumacher tie for the most titles in history with seven world championships, ahead of Juan Manuel Fangio on five.

The drivers are paid by their teams to race and have complex financial bonus structures written into their contracts regarding points, podiums, wins, and championship success. The teams themselves are paid by the Formula 1 organization, receiving a percentage of the sport's marketing revenue, a set financial prize at the end of each season depending on their championship finishing position, and various other payments determined by performance and pedigree. Teams also make money from individual sponsorship deals.

These sponsorship deals often influence the colors of the cars. While some teams use traditional racing colors (Ferrari has always raced in Italian red, for example), other teams change their paint scheme every year to suit their sponsors. The rules stipulate that both a team's cars must have the same livery so that they are easily identifiable. Teams are, however, allowed to run special liveries on both of their cars for unique races, such as anniversaries or to launch new sponsors.

Over 170 teams have competed in Formula 1 in its history. Today the limit on the number of teams permitted to enter a race is twelve. Any new team wishing to enter Formula 1 has to follow a lengthy and complex approval process and pay an entrance fee of hundreds of millions of dollars. They are then granted a license to enter the sport. New entrants can avoid this hurdle by purchasing an existing team, and this has happened often throughout history.

For example, Mercedes entered the sport in the 1950s but withdrew in the middle of the decade. To re-enter the sport many decades later they could not simply join in again, they had to buy an existing entry. Their modern story thus starts with Tyrrell, which entered Formula 1 in 1970 and sold its entry to British American Racing (BAR) in 1999. BAR was bought and its entry taken by Honda in 2006. Honda withdrew from Formula 1 at the end of 2008, and its entry was purchased by Brawn GP for 2009. Mercedes-AMG then purchased Brawn's place on the grid and has raced in F1 since 2010. When BAR bought the Tyrrell team and its F1 entry back in the late 1990s, it did so for around $50 million. Today, the minimum asking price for an F1 team and its place on the grid is estimated to be in excess of $1 billion.

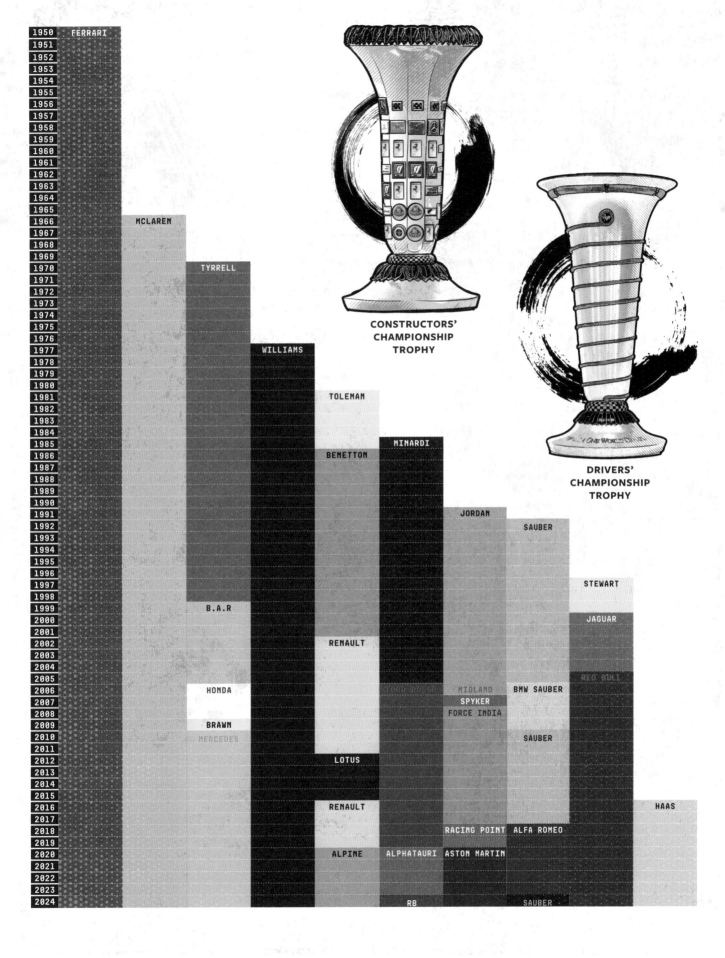

CONSTRUCTORS'
CHAMPIONSHIP
TROPHY

DRIVERS'
CHAMPIONSHIP
TROPHY

1950	FERRARI								
1951									
1952									
1953									
1954									
1955									
1956									
1957									
1958									
1959									
1960									
1961									
1962									
1963									
1964									
1965									
1966		MCLAREN							
1967									
1968									
1969									
1970			TYRRELL						
1971									
1972									
1973									
1974									
1975									
1976									
1977				WILLIAMS					
1978									
1979									
1980									
1981					TOLEMAN				
1982									
1983									
1984									
1985						MINARDI			
1986					BENETTON				
1987									
1988									
1989									
1990									
1991							JORDAN		
1992								SAUBER	
1993									
1994									
1995									
1996									
1997									STEWART
1998									
1999			B.A.R						
2000									JAGUAR
2001									
2002					RENAULT				
2003									
2004									
2005									RED BULL
2006			HONDA			TORO ROSSO	MIDLAND	BMW SAUBER	
2007							SPYKER		
2008							FORCE INDIA		
2009			BRAWN						
2010			MERCEDES					SAUBER	
2011									
2012					LOTUS				
2013									
2014									
2015									
2016					RENAULT				HAAS
2017									
2018							RACING POINT	ALFA ROMEO	
2019									
2020					ALPINE	ALPHATAURI	ASTON MARTIN		
2021									
2022									
2023									
2024						RB		SAUBER	

RACE WEEKEND FORMAT

A Grand Prix weekend takes place from Friday to Sunday and is composed of a variety of on-track sessions that range from practice to all-out competition.

Normally, the teams and drivers take part in three one-hour practice sessions, which are designed to allow them to make changes to their cars to get them as well-suited to the demands of the track as possible before entering the field of competition. Many teams use these sessions to test new developmental parts to check if they are improving the car, while also perfecting the downforce levels and setup of the cars for the drivers to feel comfortable and, of course, help them negotiate the lap as fast as possible.

With practice concluded, drivers compete to see who is the fastest over a single lap in a Saturday qualifying contest, split over three sessions. The slowest are gradually eliminated from the ongoing competition for the top-ten places on the grid. Among the twenty drivers, the order of fastest to slowest determines the order of the grid when they start the race itself, which takes place on Sunday. Drivers naturally want to start as high up the grid as possible, so that they have a better chance of scoring points or fighting for the win on Sunday. Some of the most exciting races, however, occur when a good driver in a fast car has had a poor qualifying session and has to make their way from the back of the field to the front in the Grand Prix.

For timing purposes, the racetrack is divided into three imaginary sectors, dubbed sector one, sector two, and sector three. Each car carries a sensor that triggers a timing beam at each of the junctions around the track to allow viewers an idea of how well they are doing on the lap. A green sector time denotes a personal best, and a purple sector indicates the best of anyone. Timing is taken to three decimal places, which equates to one thousandth of a second.

Teams and drivers can make aerodynamic and setup changes to their cars throughout practice sessions, but once they enter qualifying, they are banned from making any additional changes. Their cars are locked into their setup for the qualifying shootout and the race itself. Any changes made after this point can result in a driver being disadvantaged by being forced to take a penalty and drop down the grid or even start from the pitlane.

The race is known as a Grand Prix (French for "large prize"), and it is contested over a distance of around 300 km (186.4 miles). Each driver has the same allocation of tires to use throughout the weekend. In 2023, this was set at eight sets of soft, three sets of medium, and two sets of hard tires. Additionally, they receive four sets of intermediate tires (for moderately damp running) and three sets of full wet tires (for very wet running). The softer a tire, the faster it is, but the quicker it is used up. The harder a tire, the longer it lasts, but the slower it will be. Drivers can run their tires whenever they wish but must use at least two different compounds of dry tire during a Grand Prix. Usually, teams aim to make only one pitstop so that they can spend as much time racing and as little time driving slowly in the pitlane as possible. If a race is declared wet, the two-compound rule is eliminated and drivers can use any number of wet or dry tires. There is no refueling allowed during any race.

Points are awarded to the top-ten finishers of the Grand Prix: twenty-five points to the winner, then eighteen, fifteen, twelve, ten, eight, six, four, two, and one, respectively, to the next nine drivers. The driver who sets the fastest lap of the race scores an additional point, so long as they are classified in the top-ten finishers. If they are outside the top ten, nobody gets the point.

Some race weekends are run on a "sprint format" designed to increase the number of competitive sessions.

Drivers and their teams score the same number of points, and if a driver changes teams midseason, the driver keeps their points—and so does the team with whom they scored them. Team points stay with the team and do not transition with the driver.

STANDARD FORMAT

FRIDAY

Two practice sessions of one hour

One practice session of one hour

One qualifying session of one hour

Q1
Fastest fifteen advance. Positions sixteen to twenty locked in.

Q2
Fastest ten advance. Positions eleven to fifteen locked in.

Q3
Top-ten shootout. Positions one to ten locked in.

SUNDAY

GRAND PRIX
(300 km minimum, 305 km maximum except for Monaco 260 km minimum. Races unstopped maximum time of two hours, or three hours including stoppages.)

SPRINT FORMAT

FRIDAY

One practice session of one hour

Sprint qualifying session of one hour (same format as standard Saturday qualifying but with shorter sessions)

SATURDAY

SPRINT
100km race with grid formed from Sprint qualifying

Grand Prix qualifying (same format as standard Saturday qualifying)

SUNDAY

GRAND PRIX
(Same as standard Grand Prix weekend.)

MODERN CAR REGULATIONS

Formula 1 teams are known as constructors, which means, by definition, they have to "construct" their own cars. So while they are permitted to purchase engines, gearboxes, and some other specific parts, the cars themselves have to be designed and created by each team individually. Thousands of unique pieces go into every car, from the bodywork that you can see down to all the internal parts that you can't. Because of this, every car is bespoke, singularly unique to that team.

Modern Formula 1 cars are the largest in history, with regulations stating they must be no wider than 200 cm (6.5 feet) and no taller than 95 cm (3 feet). While there is no specified limit on the length of the car, the maximum distance between the front and rear wheels is limited to 360 cm (11.8 feet), and as such, car lengths tend not to vary much.

The car must have only four wheels—which sounds obvious, but some F1 cars have run six wheels in the past! Also, only the rear wheels are permitted to be driven, and the front wheels are solely for steering. Four-wheel drive is therefore not permitted.

The chassis of the car must contain a survival cell, into which the driver sits and is secured to a removable seat molded to their specific body using a six-point harness. Every car must feature a roll hoop and halo cockpit protection device. The engine is attached to the rear of the survival cell, along with an eight-forward and one-reverse gear transmission.

Formula 1 cars have for decades been notable for their use of wings and complex aerodynamics, which is the art of using airflow to push a car downward and create grip. Since 2022, however, car design has limited the use of wings to produce downforce. F1 cars today utilize not only wings and aerodynamics on the visible surfaces of the car, but also ground effect via tunnels under the car that create areas of low pressure that suck the cars downward to produce the same grip. This ensures that airflow over the car (known as dirty air) receives as little disruption as possible so that the car behind can follow closely. All cars are fitted with a drag reduction system (DRS), which opens a slot in the rear wing to reduce drag and increase straight-line speed to aid overtaking, when chasing cars are within a second of the car ahead.

Modern Formula 1 engines are 1.6-liter, V6 turbo-hybrid units, limited to 15,000 revolutions per minute (rpm) with a power output estimated to be between 750 and 1,000 horsepower. Fuel injection is limited to 500 bar, with fuel limited to 110 kg (242.5 lbs) per race and fuel flow limited to a rate of 100 kg/h (220.5 lbs) above 10,500 rpm.

Modern turbo-hybrid power units are composed of more than just the engine, however, as they must also have a turbocharger, a motor generator unit kinetic (MGU-K, which harnesses energy under braking), a motor generator unit heat (MGU-H, which harnesses energy as heat in the exhaust), an energy store such as a battery (which holds the regenerated energy), and a control electronics unit (which operates the entire system). Drivers can use a maximum of four of each over a full season, and eight of the four parts that make up an exhaust system. If they go over their allocation, grid penalties are applied after qualifying for the race where they have gone over the limit.

Together, the car and driver must weigh a minimum of 798 kg (1,759 lbs). Officials check that the car is within the regulations at the start of each race weekend by setting each one on a special weigh bridge to check that both its dimensions and weight are correct. They can call the car back to be weighed at any point over the race weekend, and cars are weighed and checked for legality after the race as well.

Refueling has been banned in Formula 1 for over a decade, and so the 110 kg (242.5 lbs) of road legal fuel must last an entire Grand Prix distance. A specimen of fuel is taken from the car after the Grand Prix has finished to ensure that it complies with regulations.

Formula 1 wheel rims must be fitted with Pirelli's eighteen-inch P Zero Formula 1 tires, which have a total diameter of 28.3 inches. Rear tires are wider than front tires to provide greater grip to the car's driven rear axle.

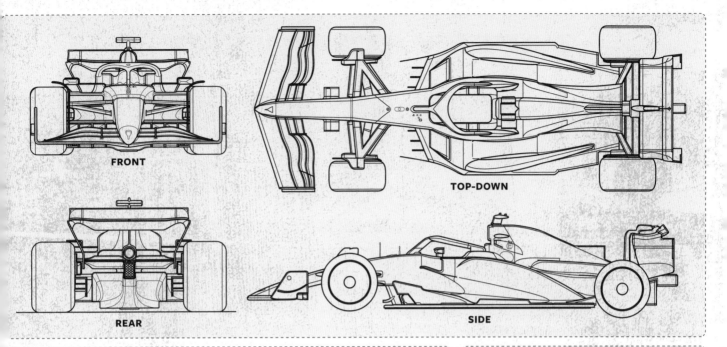

FRONT

TOP-DOWN

REAR

SIDE

POWER UNIT

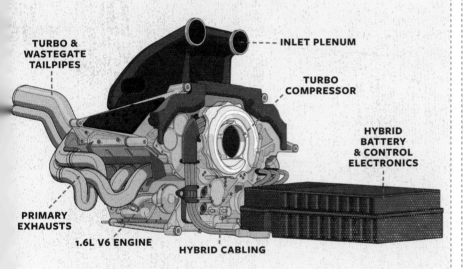

TURBO & WASTEGATE TAILPIPES

INLET PLENUM

TURBO COMPRESSOR

HYBRID BATTERY & CONTROL ELECTRONICS

PRIMARY EXHAUSTS

1.6L V6 ENGINE

HYBRID CABLING

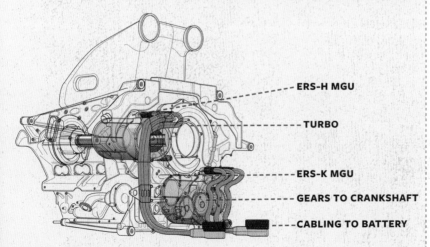

ERS-H MGU

TURBO

ERS-K MGU

GEARS TO CRANKSHAFT

CABLING TO BATTERY

STEERING WHEEL

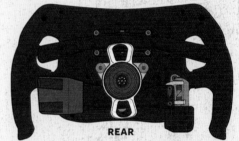

REAR

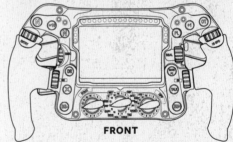

FRONT

A Formula 1 steering wheel is more than just a means to turn the front wheels. The sheer number of buttons, dials, toggles, and switches means that many hundreds of options can be operated from this device to affect all manner of intricate car setup details. A driver has to memorize where to access these options, since during the intensity of the race, they cannot spare a split second to look down at the screen. Gears are changed using paddles behind the wheel, which also has a hand-operated clutch, but these are by far the simplest actions on what has become a complex computer more than a simple directional device.

SAFETY EQUIPMENT

For the past seventy years, innovation and regulation have had lasting effects on the safety of Formula 1 cars. While motor racing, due to the high speeds, will never be 100 percent safe, modern F1 cars are designed to include a number of features to protect the driver in case of an accident.

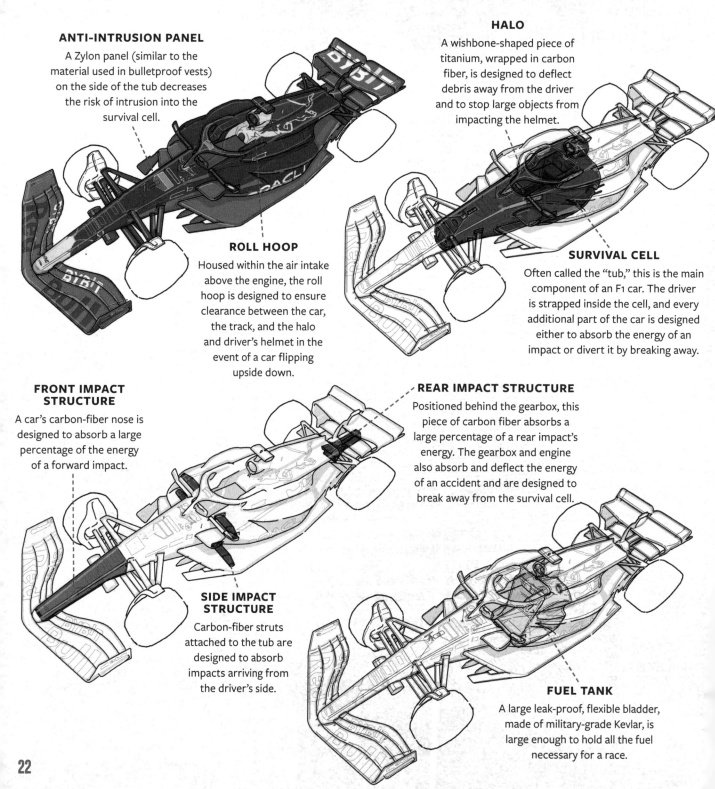

ANTI-INTRUSION PANEL

A Zylon panel (similar to the material used in bulletproof vests) on the side of the tub decreases the risk of intrusion into the survival cell.

HALO

A wishbone-shaped piece of titanium, wrapped in carbon fiber, is designed to deflect debris away from the driver and to stop large objects from impacting the helmet.

ROLL HOOP

Housed within the air intake above the engine, the roll hoop is designed to ensure clearance between the car, the track, and the halo and driver's helmet in the event of a car flipping upside down.

SURVIVAL CELL

Often called the "tub," this is the main component of an F1 car. The driver is strapped inside the cell, and every additional part of the car is designed either to absorb the energy of an impact or divert it by breaking away.

FRONT IMPACT STRUCTURE

A car's carbon-fiber nose is designed to absorb a large percentage of the energy of a forward impact.

REAR IMPACT STRUCTURE

Positioned behind the gearbox, this piece of carbon fiber absorbs a large percentage of a rear impact's energy. The gearbox and engine also absorb and deflect the energy of an accident and are designed to break away from the survival cell.

SIDE IMPACT STRUCTURE

Carbon-fiber struts attached to the tub are designed to absorb impacts arriving from the driver's side.

FUEL TANK

A large leak-proof, flexible bladder, made of military-grade Kevlar, is large enough to hold all the fuel necessary for a race.

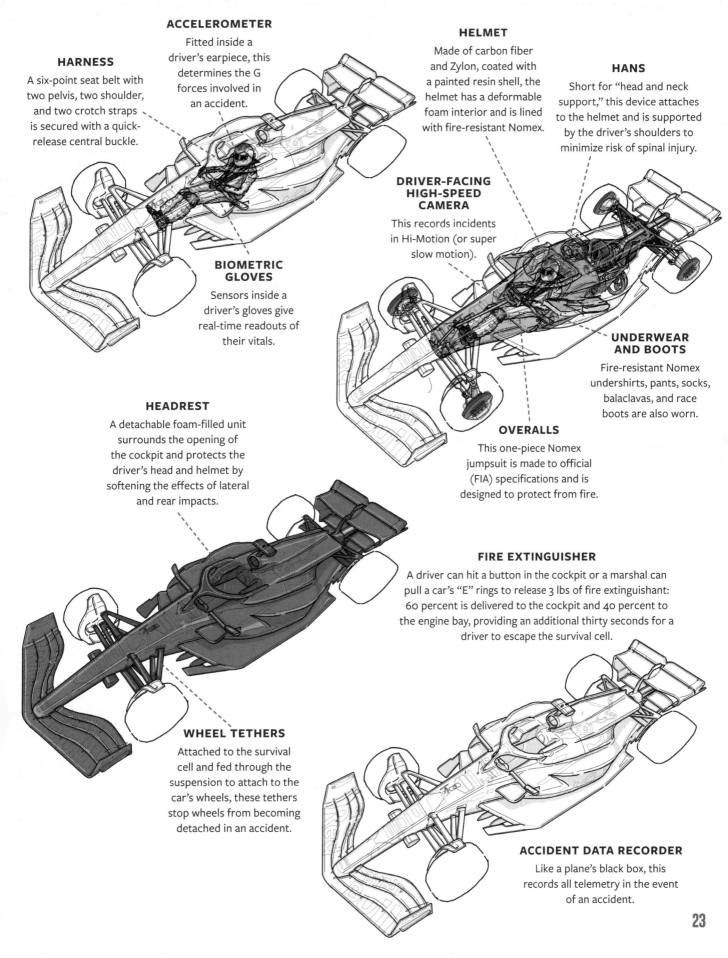

HARNESS
A six-point seat belt with two pelvis, two shoulder, and two crotch straps is secured with a quick-release central buckle.

ACCELEROMETER
Fitted inside a driver's earpiece, this determines the G forces involved in an accident.

HELMET
Made of carbon fiber and Zylon, coated with a painted resin shell, the helmet has a deformable foam interior and is lined with fire-resistant Nomex.

HANS
Short for "head and neck support," this device attaches to the helmet and is supported by the driver's shoulders to minimize risk of spinal injury.

DRIVER-FACING HIGH-SPEED CAMERA
This records incidents in Hi-Motion (or super slow motion).

BIOMETRIC GLOVES
Sensors inside a driver's gloves give real-time readouts of their vitals.

UNDERWEAR AND BOOTS
Fire-resistant Nomex undershirts, pants, socks, balaclavas, and race boots are also worn.

HEADREST
A detachable foam-filled unit surrounds the opening of the cockpit and protects the driver's head and helmet by softening the effects of lateral and rear impacts.

OVERALLS
This one-piece Nomex jumpsuit is made to official (FIA) specifications and is designed to protect from fire.

FIRE EXTINGUISHER
A driver can hit a button in the cockpit or a marshal can pull a car's "E" rings to release 3 lbs of fire extinguishant: 60 percent is delivered to the cockpit and 40 percent to the engine bay, providing an additional thirty seconds for a driver to escape the survival cell.

WHEEL TETHERS
Attached to the survival cell and fed through the suspension to attach to the car's wheels, these tethers stop wheels from becoming detached in an accident.

ACCIDENT DATA RECORDER
Like a plane's black box, this records all telemetry in the event of an accident.

DESIGNING, DEVELOPING, AND TESTING

Modern-day Formula 1 leaves almost nothing to chance. Every element of a car's performance is monitored and analyzed in real time both at the track and at a team's factory. Each car carries around three hundred sensors, sending back over a terabyte of performance-based information every race weekend. Over an entire season, a team collects more than 10 billion data points. Every one of these is studied in an effort to find an advantage, resolve an issue, and create the ultimate F1 car.

Cars are designed using CAD (computer-aided design) technology, which replaced hand drawing many decades ago. These digital designs create virtual cars whose aerodynamic philosophies are tested using CFD (computational fluid dynamics), a mathematical science that predicts fluid flow around any given object. Car designs are simultaneously tested in a wind tunnel, into which a 60-percent-size model is placed to provide real airflow analysis.

The real car, once built, can be tested in the factory on a seven-post rig, which replicates the real-world forces the car will undergo by mimicking the lateral and longitudinal changes in weight transfer experienced at any specific track. Known also as a "shaker," the rig replicates the specific curbs employed at different tracks, the bumps to be found on circuits, and the many directional forces the suspension will be forced to travel in competition and at full speeds.

This is how Formula 1 cars, and their developmental parts, are designed and tested. But under the sport's many regulations, the amount of time teams can spend putting their designs through wind tunnel or CFD testing is restricted. The lower down the championship ladder a team finds itself, the more time it has available. The world champions therefore have less time than anyone else to get things right.

But no matter how brilliant a team's designers or how good a car looks in the virtual world, there is still no guarantee that the car and its developmental parts will work as planned when they hit the track. The only true test comes when cars are raced for real. And, again, the amount of time available to test new parts is restricted.

New cars are traditionally launched in January or February, and the first race of a new season usually takes place in March. This means there is now just one three-day pre-season test at which teams and drivers are allowed to get to grips with their new creations before the season begins. The pre-season test is an event at which all teams gather to run their new cars on the same track at the same time. They can only run one car per team, so drivers must share track time between them, but over the three-day test, they have around twenty-five total hours of track time to use as they see fit.

Once the season begins, teams can only run their current cars and test new developments on a Grand Prix weekend. The only testing permitted outside race weekends is to aid the sport's tire partner in developing their tires, not for teams to develop their cars. This is to both save costs and to ensure that the big teams can't gain an advantage by testing more often than their smaller rivals. That said, teams are allowed to run cars more than two years old as often as they like, since the rate of development in Formula 1 is so fast that a two-year-old car is deemed to be competitively obsolete.

Drivers can, however, get a taste for development parts by spending time on a simulator. The most advanced units cost many millions of dollars and have become some of the most heavily protected secrets in the sport, as the best can accurately replicate the changes in car performance any single development will make. They also form an excellent training tool to keep racers driving outside race weekends.

With real-world testing so limited, the importance of data is key to modern Formula 1. Teams must correlate what they see in the virtual world on CFD, in their wind tunnels, and on simulators to what they see in the real world on track to ensure a Formula 1 car is developed efficiently throughout a season.

FLAGS AND SAFETY CARS

In motorsport, the quickest way to get a message to the drivers is through the use of trackside flags. Drivers are taught from their earliest racing days to always keep a watchful eye for flags, and although today these warnings are delivered via notifications on their steering wheels and on LED panels around the track, the physical flags themselves still take precedence as the official notification system. The only time that lights take precedence is at race start, when the gantry above the start line tells the drivers that the race is beginning. Five lights illuminate, and when they are extinguished, the race begins.

The safety car, also known as a pace car, is used in motor racing to slow the field down in the event of a major incident on track. Its purpose is to allow trackside marshals to clear an incident or for medical crews to attend the scene of an accident without suspending the race under a red flag. In Formula 1, the safety car is also used in wet-weather conditions to slow down the field and ensure that the race continues under caution until conditions are considered suitable to resume the race. In the event of a red flag and race suspension for poor weather, the safety car is also used to trial conditions on its own, to determine whether they are suitable for the race to be restarted.

There is also a medical car in which the race's official medical delegate rides. This is outfitted with essential medical equipment to be used at the scene of an accident. If only one area of the track is deemed to be at temporarily high risk, a virtual safety car (VSC) can be called. In that case, no physical safety car enters the track, and instead a slower laptime is enforced so that drivers pass the risk-affected area at a reduced speed.

GREEN

Session has begun. If shown after a yellow flag, the track ahead is clear. Resume race speed.

YELLOW

Hazard ahead. Slow down.

DOUBLE YELLOW

Track blocked ahead. Slow down and be prepared to stop.

YELLOW ALONG WITH THE WHITE SC BOARD

Slow down, a safety car is deployed.

YELLOW AND RED STRIPES

Debris/fluid is on track.

RED

Session stopped. Slow down and return to the pits.

CHECKERED

End of session.

BLUE

Faster car approaching behind. Be prepared to let them pass.

WHITE

Slow vehicle ahead.

BLACK WITH ORANGE CIRCLE

Return to pits immediately for repairs.

BLACK/WHITE

Warning for unsportsmanlike conduct.

BLACK

You have been disqualified.

TIRES

Tires are critically important to Formula 1. They represent the four points of contact where the full power of the car meets the road. Having the right tire for the right scenario is crucial to a good race.

In modern Formula 1, there is a range of six dry-weather tires, with C0 being the hardest and C5 the softest. For each race weekend, three of the six compounds are chosen and named the red-walled "soft," the yellow-branded "medium," and the white-denoted "hard" options for the race weekend. The softer a tire, the stickier and grippier it is. With more grip, the tire is faster but also used up more quickly. The hard tire lasts longer but produces slower laptimes. The medium sits in the middle. The teams determine their race strategies to use at least two of these compounds in order to get from lights out to checkered flag the fastest. There are also two designations of wet-weather tires, the green-marked "intermediate" for light rain and the blue side-walled "wet" tire for heavier precipitation.

Drivers describe the need to keep tires "in the window," which means the perfect conditions for a tire to be at its maximum effectiveness. This usually relates to the temperature of the tire during the race. Tires that are overworked through aggressive driving will overheat. But if a driver goes too easy, the tires will lose temperature. Thus, tires need to be kept within a specific operating "window."

Dry tires are kept in heated blankets before they are put onto the car in the garage or at a pitstop, so that they can be kept as close to the perfect operating temperature as possible. This luxury is not permitted for the two types of wet-weather tires, which must go on to the car at ambient temperature.

Today, Formula 1 uses just one tire manufacturer, but over its history, there have been nine different suppliers. At various points in the sport's history, multiple tire companies have competed against one another, adding an extra element of intrigue to the complexities of race strategy and competition.

PIRELLI 1950–1958, 1981–1986, 1989–1991, 2011–today

FIRESTONE 1950–1960, 1966–1975

DUNLOP 1950–1970, 1976–1977

ENGLEBERT 1950–1958

CONTINENTAL 1954–1955, 1958

AVON 1954, 1956–1959, 1981–1982

GOODYEAR 1964–1998

BRIDGESTONE 1976–1977, 1997–2010

MICHELIN 1977–1984, 2001–2006

TRAINING

It may not look like it from the outside, but Formula 1 is one of the most physically demanding and extreme sports in the world. F1 drivers require leg, arm, and extreme core strength; aerobic conditioning; balance; and incredible stamina and endurance. Their training and diet are unique, not just within sport, but within motor racing.

Strapped tight into the cockpit, the driver maintains a racing position similar to lying in the bath and resting your feet on the taps. Core strength is therefore key. Drivers also have to train their legs, particularly their left leg, for the huge forces required not only to engage the carbon brakes (about 350 lbs of pressure) but to maintain enough feel to modify their application by mere millimeters. A driver's neck also requires strength conditioning, as it has to hold up the combined weight of a racer's head and helmet under the more than two Gs of acceleration and sometimes more than six Gs of deceleration. Cornering can see sustained forces in excess of five Gs, with changes of direction switching the direction of force in an instant.

A driver's heart rate will often average more than 175 bpm during a Grand Prix, and in warmer races, heat can exceed 40 degrees Celsius (104 degrees Fahrenheit), with racers clothed in fire-resistant overalls and underwear. As such, they can lose over 4 kg (9 lbs) in body weight due to the intense perspiration their bodies experience. Such a huge loss of weight and fluids, in turn, affects cognitive function.

Drivers, therefore, spend a lot of time in the gym building up their muscles to endure the forces sustained in an F1 car, with machines designed specifically to train the most-used muscles in the neck, legs, and forearms. Cardio plays a key role in training, too, with drivers engaging in many endurance sports outside race weekends, such as triathlons. F1 drivers tend to have the body composition of endurance athletes, being light but strong. In order to stop racers from attempting to hit unhealthy targets for weight, however, a minimum has been set in Formula 1 for a driver and their seat to weigh no less than 80 kg (176.4 lbs).

Drivers engage the services of personal trainers, who become a key component of their daily lives, overseeing not just their gym routines but also their sleep patterns and diet. F1 drivers eat and live clean, basing their diets around poultry, fish, vegetables, and clean carbs.

While they often allow themselves a cheat meal after a race and a few glasses of champagne after a podium, alcohol and junk food are, for the most part, strictly off limits.

TRAVEL AND FREIGHT

Formula 1 visits more than twenty locations over the course of a ten-month season. The sheer number of races means that turnaround times are often tight between events, with some held on concurrent weekends—occasionally there are three races being held in three countries on three successive weekends. As such, the smooth execution of the transportation of the equipment that teams need is a vital aspect of the world championship challenge.

To facilitate their travel, teams have a minimum of five sets of everything they need to set up their garages, pit walls, and hospitality areas. These sets rotate around the world in a complex dance, with one set often staying in one geographical area. In order to reduce cost, teams use both sea and air freight for long-haul races, while in Europe, they use trucks to transport their gear from race to race.

For European races, the paddock and garage areas start to be packed down during the Grand Prix itself, such that by Sunday evening almost three hundred trucks will be on the move to the next location to enable starting the new build on Tuesday. For these few races, that includes the motorhomes that house the teams, which are created from the trucks themselves, piecing together the rear sections like a giant game of Tetris.

For international races, the contents of the garages and hospitality areas are placed inside specially designed freight containers, which are made to fit perfectly inside the six or more Boeing 747s allocated by Formula 1 partner DHL for their transportation. Each team has three special pallets for priority items, and then of course, there are the cars themselves. The most important part of the team's operation has to fly from race to race, since each chassis is unique. Updated parts are flown out specifically on a race-to-race basis.

In total, over five hundred tons of equipment are transported each year by sea and more than six hundred tons by air, for a total global journey of just under 93,000 miles. Should the teams find a weekend free between events, everything is brought home to their factories to be checked, repaired if necessary, repainted, repacked, and sent back on its way to the next race weekend. The organization of the freight transportation is an essential job that requires military precision and hundreds of members of staff across the teams, DHL, and F1 itself to keep the sport up and running.

FIA AND FORMULA 1

The Fédération Internationale de l'Automobile (FIA) has overseen the running of the Formula 1 World Championship from its inception. Today, it is responsible for the sport's regulation, which falls under three distinct categories and comprises three rule books. These run to many hundreds of pages each and are, for those interested, available to view on the FIA's website.

The technical regulations outline the parameters by which all Formula 1 cars must be designed, which ranges from the chassis to engine and tires and includes every rule relating to manufacturing. The sporting regulations outline how events are run and include everything from race weekend format to the rules of every practice session, qualifying format, and the race, along with on-track racing rules. In addition to this, the FIA's International Sporting Code is the code of conduct to be followed by all racing championships. Finally, there are financial regulations, which are new as of the 2020s. In order to rein in the huge amounts of money being spent on the sport, and to stop major manufacturers from having an unfair advantage over smaller independent teams, a "budget cap" was introduced at the start of the sport's seventh decade. These rules detail how much money teams can spend and exactly what they are permitted to spend money on. The FIA is responsible for policing all regulations and imposing penalties for any infractions.

On race weekends, the most important FIA department is Race Control, which includes the race director, race stewards, and a dedicated team of technical delegates. This team oversees the competitive operation of the weekend, from ensuring that cars are within regulations to the use of flags, deployment of the safety car, and the issuing of any penalties for race incidents. The FIA is also responsible for safety at F1 races. To be granted a license to host a Formula 1 race, all circuits must meet strict criteria related to runoff, barriers, fencing, and the latest medical facilities. An FIA medical delegate and FIA doctors attend every race, and the governing body is active in its training of the trackside marshals, who attend every event as volunteers to keep the drivers and fans safe. The FIA is also responsible for accrediting print and online written media.

The composition of the FIA is complex and includes numerous committees and councils specializing in different aspects of both motorsport and civilian transportation. The FIA is also the first point of arbitration for any misdemeanors and appeals over subsequent penalties.

Formula 1, known for many years as Formula 1 Management, deals with the promotional and commercial side of the sport. It is Formula 1's job to organize the race calendar, which the FIA then approves; Formula 1 also oversees the handing out of prize money to the teams based on their championship finishing position. F1 is also responsible for helping teams to organize the transportation of their freight, for overseeing the allocation and distribution of team and guest passes, and for organizing security at events.

One of Formula 1's biggest responsibilities is creating a live global television feed of every race weekend. Formula 1 negotiates broadcast deals with networks around the world along with their accreditation. Formula 1 also started its own digital television network, F1 TV, in the late 2010s, and alongside this there is a comprehensive digital division that creates one of the world's fastest-growing and most-followed sources of sports digital and social media content. Formula 1 employs a communications and marketing department to help promote the sport and engage new audiences, negotiates licensing opportunities, and oversees the running of the VIP Paddock Club.

A DRIVER'S ROUTE TO FORMULA 1

In 2014, the FIA devised a "Global Pathway" from karting to Formula 1, designed to simplify and streamline the route young drivers can take to reach the pinnacle of open wheel racing. At each stage the power and the complexity of the car increase to give young drivers the tools they require to proceed in their racing career.

Most racing drivers today begin their careers in **KARTING**, starting at the junior national level and rising to the major international races and championships (those approved by the FIA and the Commission Internationale de Karting, CIK). Most children will begin their careers before their tenth birthday and race into their teens before they become eligible to race in single-seaters.

After karting, racers usually progress into open wheel by racing in **FORMULA 4**, which is national class racing that begins at age fifteen. Championships feature a 1.4- to 2.0-liter, inline-four engine from a single provider, powering a simple slicks and wings single-seater.

Next on the ladder is **FORMULA REGIONAL**, a set of regional, rather than national, single-seater championships, utilizing Formula 3 machinery featuring a spec 2.0-liter engine and spec chassis with a six-speed semiautomatic gearbox.

The **FIA FORMULA 3 CHAMPIONSHIP** follows, and it is an international one-make (spec) series that takes place on Formula 1 weekends. Drivers are eligible to compete from the age of sixteen, and all use the same drag-reduction-system-enabled Dallara chassis, Mecachrome normally aspirated V6 engine with a top speed of 300 kph (186 mph), and Pirelli tires. The cars are designed to mimic small versions of 2017 Formula 1 cars with the addition of ground-effect-style floors.

The final step on the ladder has been known in the past as Formula 2, Formula 3000, and GP2. Today, the **FIA FORMULA 2 CHAMPIONSHIP** is an international spec series held on Formula 1 weekends with drivers over the age of seventeen all using the same DRS-enabled Dallara chassis, Mecachrome 3.4-liter turbocharged engine (using synthetic sustainable fuel), with a top speed of 335 kph (208 mph), and F1-style 18-inch Pirelli tires. The championship will use a brand-new car from 2024, built to mimic the latest F1 designs and to pass 2024 FIA F1 safety standards and to comply with new specifications in terms of braking, steering effort, and ergonomics to accommodate a wide range of drivers in making the championship as accessible as possible.

Success at each level leads to the granting of a license to race at a higher level, in addition to earning points for championship-finishing position that go toward the granting of the ultimate goal: a Formula 1 Super License. This verifies that a driver is of sufficient experience and quality to race in Formula 1. A driver requires at least forty Super License points to be granted the right to race in Formula 1, and they will achieve all forty for finishing in the top three championship positions in Formula 2. Thirty points are awarded for winning the Formula 3 championship, eighteen for Formula Regional, and twelve for Formula 4. Other than the top three in F2, the only other driver to which an automatic Super License is granted is America's IndyCar champion.

FIA
FORMULA 1
WORLD
CHAMPIONSHIP

FIA
FORMULA 2
CHAMPIONSHIP

FIA FORMULA
3 CHAMPIONSHIP

FORMULA REGIONAL

FORMULA 4

KARTING

OTHER RACING

While this book is about Formula 1, there are many other incredible forms of racing that take place all over the world. These championships represent some of the most competitive and exciting motorsport championships outside of F1, and they are racing goals in their own right. Competing in them and scoring well, however, can also lead to the awarding of F1 Super License points, such that champion drivers outside Formula 1 might be afforded the chance to switch disciplines.

INDYCAR

The pinnacle of American open wheel racing, IndyCar has existed in one form or another since 1920. Today, it is one of the closest and most exhilarating forms of single-seater competition in the world thanks in large part to its standardized use of one Dallara chassis and just a few engine suppliers (Honda and Chevrolet as of 2024). The championship races on road, street, and oval tracks, with its biggest draw being the annual Indy 500, which has existed for almost 110 years. Although IndyCar drivers don't need Super License points to race in the championship, the top ten drivers in the championship receive Super License points, and the champion gains the forty points required to race in F1. IndyCar has its own feeder series path, known as the "Road to Indy," with staged leaps in performance similar to the FIA's "Global Pathway" to F1.

FORMULA E

An all-electric open wheel international championship, Formula E competes on temporary street circuits built in some of the world's major cities. Standard chassis are used by all teams, and manufacturers are able to develop the powertrain and software. The top ten drivers receive Super License points, with the world champion receiving thirty.

NASCAR

The National Association for Stock Car Auto Racing (NASCAR), has its roots in the moonshine runners in Prohibition-era America in the 1920s, who modified road cars to escape the police. The championship today races "stock" cars, using race versions of production road cars on road and oval tracks. The NASCAR season has over thirty races a year exclusively in the United States and is one of the most popular forms of racing in America. The top eight drivers score F1 Super License points, with the champion taking home fifteen.

ENDURANCE

Formerly known as Sportscar racing, Endurance racing is the art of a group of drivers racing in turns as co-pilots to cover the farthest distance in a set number of hours on a race circuit. The most famous race on the schedule is the 24 Hours of Le Mans, which forms the centerpiece of the World Endurance Championship (WEC). For many years the cars had to be production models that you could buy, but over recent decades into the 2000s, the top class was for special prototype cars. Today, the top class of endurance racing is the Hypercar division, with rules brought in to align the international WEC and American IMSA (International Motor Sports Association) class. The top ten WEC drivers receive F1 Super License points, with the top eight gaining points in IMSA and the champions gaining thirty and eighteen points per championship.

TOURING CARS

National Touring Car championships have existed since the beginning of motor racing and have moved from standard road-going cars to modified racing versions of road cars. The most famous are the German championship, known as DTM (Deutsche Tourenwagen Masters), and Australian Supercars division. Drivers of these championships also qualify for Super License points.

RALLY

Rallying involves point-to-point driving on closed sections of road, and it is held around the world on asphalt, dirt, sand, and ice courses. This is not circuit racing (like most other forms of racing) since it involves individual time trials. There is a World Rally Championship and many famous individual races, such as the Dakar Rally and Baja 1000. These events don't count for Super License points.

FACTORY

ASTON MARTIN

Opened in 2023, the AMR Technology Campus is the most modern purpose built F1 factory in the world. Located next to the Silverstone circuit and home to over eight hundred staff, the three buildings and full site cover an area of 400,000 square feet.

Every facet of the team's operation is housed on site, with the exception of the team's current power units that are built by Mercedes in nearby Brixworth. In 2026, the team will become a full works team with HRC (Honda) powertrains.

The two largest departments are the team's design office and manufacturing and machining divisions, with each occupying half a floor of the main building. Alongside them are the electronics department and trim shops, inspection team, IT department, logistics and a commercial and marketing group, management offices for the top brass, and an impressive lobby and trophy room. Effective in late 2024, there will be a restaurant and gym for staff to use.

MANUFACTURING

Since all teams are necessitated by regulation to be constructors, each team must build the majority of their cars' components themselves. And no matter how far advanced technology becomes, there will always be the need for artisans and craftspeople. These uniquely skilled members of the team work within the manufacturing (also called fabrication) department, tasked with building parts as varied as the complex exhaust systems and the intricate carbon fiber designs of the bodywork and floor.

WIND TUNNEL

One of the most important instruments in determining the design of a Formula 1 car, the wind tunnel is a large cylinder that features a giant fan at one end. A 60-percent-size model of the team's car is placed in this tunnel, often on a rolling road, with air pushed over the car to replicate the direction of air travel over the contours of the design at racing speeds. Analysis of the airflow tells the team whether their designs are achieving the desired aerodynamic effect.

RACE BAYS

From the very first F1 team base all the way through to today, one thing they all have in common is the race bay. These are the areas where the cars take their first breaths as their engines are fired up; where they are first built and are returned to be taken apart, examined, repaired, and rebuilt. Essentially a larger version of a team's garage space at races, the race bay is a car's home, from where it departs for a race and to whence it returns.

MISSION CONTROL

With terabytes of data being sent from racetrack to factory every weekend, live and during every session, mission control is the beating heart of a Formula 1 team. And while there is a team at the track keeping an eye on every parameter it can, mission control is where alerts are often first noted and issues detected. Think of NASA's mission control at Cape Canaveral or the Johnson Space Center, and you're not far off. With the exception, perhaps, that these rooms deal with more information in a shorter amount of time. They are the absolute hub of data analysis and can influence everything from race strategy to the decision to retire a car before an engine expires.

GARAGE

At every Grand Prix, the teams are given garage space to set up their own personal working environments. Housed within their garage allocations are areas to store all the essentials that the team needs to operate, from fuel to tires and almost all spare parts. The garage forms the IT hub of operations for the weekend, with radios and headphones stored and operated for each team member, telemetry from the cars beamed back to the screens in the main garage itself as well as to banks of monitors behind the garage walls, the engineering offices, and the factory. Fuel suppliers have a dedicated area where they can test fuel samples to determine engine wear rates by checking for microscopic shards of engine material in the fuel or oil.

The garage itself is a hive of activity, as it is here where all car setup changes are made and any issues with the cars fixed. Each car has its own bay, where it

can be fully taken apart and reassembled if necessary. Each driver has their own team of mechanics and engineers, and they have their own dedicated area to keep personal effects and store their helmets.

With so many guests and VIPs attending races, most F1 garages today feature a viewing area at the rear, so that sponsors and guests can get a real-time view of the team's work during a session.

The pit wall is where the key members of the team sit during sessions and make the calls that affect the race. They each have banks of monitors to watch, and they can radio other members of the team and the drivers in the cockpits. At Ferrari, the seating is arranged like this: Race Engineer Driver 1 / Sporting Director / Team Principal / Head of Track Engineering / Head of Strategy / Race Engineer Driver 2

PITSTOP

Pitstops are a key moment in every race. Per regulations, every driver must make at least one pitstop in dry conditions in order to have raced on at least two different compounds of slick tire. Any time lost is a severe disadvantage, so pitstops can win or lose a race. Today, more than twenty members of a team are involved in every pitstop in order to service the car as quickly as possible and send it on its way.

Red Bull Racing has, for many years, been the benchmark team for pitstops. With the old thirteen-inch tires, they set a then world record at the 2019 Brazilian Grand Prix for a full four-wheel change in 1.82 seconds. With the new eighteen-inch wheels proving much heavier, pitstop times were expected to become slower. But teams are still achieving sub-two-second stops, with Red Bull still the best over a season, but McLaren holding the world record of 1.80 seconds at the time of publication.

So how does Red Bull do it?

Once the car stops on its marks, the front and rear jackmen hoist the car up to raise the wheels

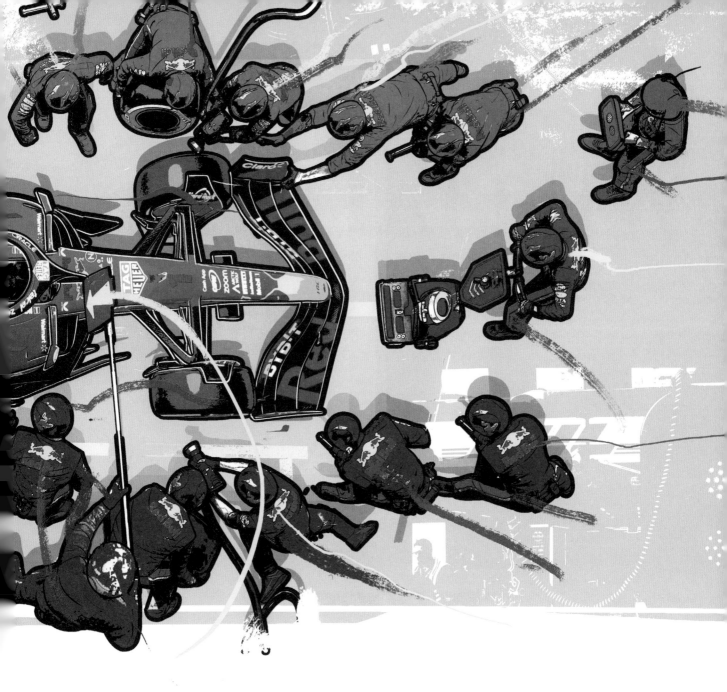

off the ground. As they do this, four gunners attach their wheel guns to the central wheel nuts to detach them, with one crew member per wheel tasked with removing the old tire. As soon as it has been removed, another crew member on each corner of the car puts on a new wheel, with the gunner then tightening the new wheel nut in place. Two crew members hold the car steady to stop it rocking, while at the front, two team members have preloaded electric screwdrivers ready to adjust wing levels while the wheels are being changed. There are crew members standing by with spare front and rear jacks if the primaries fail, with one crew member waiting at the rear with a starter in case the car stalls. In very rare examples, a member of the crew might also have a spare steering wheel, should there be an issue with the one the driver is using. There are also crew members tasked with removing and replacing a nose and front wing in the event it is damaged. Once the work is completed, the car is dropped back to the track and goes on its way. And all in under two seconds.

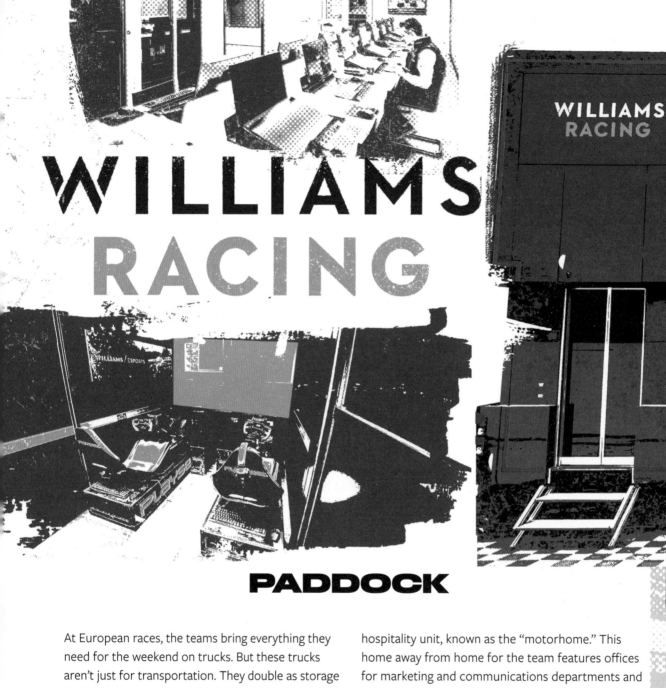

WILLIAMS RACING

PADDOCK

At European races, the teams bring everything they need for the weekend on trucks. But these trucks aren't just for transportation. They double as storage facilities on the weekend, and the double-decker units are also used as offices. Not only that, but they operate as foundations for an elevated engineering hub, known as the "tree house."

Williams Racing uses four trucks over the weekend to house their spare parts and offices and create the footing for their tree house. The engineering room is set out so as to give the team the perfect working environment to coordinate strategy.

On the opposite side of the paddock, the trucks are used in a giant game of Tetris to build a

hospitality unit, known as the "motorhome." This home away from home for the team features offices for marketing and communications departments and team management, along with special rooms for the drivers to relax in. The ground floor is a dedicated area for visitors to be welcomed and fed, with a large kitchen area out the back cooking restaurant-quality food throughout the day. VIP guests of the team and drivers have their own area on the first floor alongside a simulator room to drive the track in the virtual world. On the second floor, a roof deck features comfortable seating and one of the best views of the track and paddock, served by a well-stocked bar.

INTERNATIONAL BROADCAST

Graphic Operators

Main Director

Edito Direc

Graphic Producers

OBC Director

Repla Direc

Replay Operators

Producer

Prod

Replay Operators

Media Engineering

F1 is renowned as the pinnacle of global motorsport, and that excellence is reflected in the incredible world-leading broadcast that brings the sport to an audience of one and a half billion people in 180 territories. From the second you hear the stirring, Brian Tyler–composed F1 theme music during a race weekend broadcast on any one of the seventy-four global broadcast partners to the display of the final finishing positions at the end of the session, everything you see is directed and produced by Formula 1's in-house "world feed" international broadcast team.

There are two main hubs of operation. The Media and Technology Center (M&TC), located at Biggin Hill in England, deploys the largest remote production system in the world. One hundred and forty personnel bring together 120 concurrent live video streams from the track, where the Event Technical Center (ETC) is located. With 750 pieces of equipment on site and seventy-five staff members, the ETC is built within the circuit confines ten days before each event.

The teams at the track and back in England are led by a front bench of producers and directors who conduct a visual and audio concerto of ultimate sporting excitement, using timing, graphics, replays, and team radio to add to the drama.

Five hundred terabytes of data are transferred every race weekend, which is more than fifty times the annual total created by NASA's Hubble Space Telescope. The footage is broadcast live from a total of ninety on-board cameras, with a maximum of seven on each car. Twenty-eight trackside cameras and two pit wall cameras cover all the race action, eight free roaming camera operators capture events in pitlane and in the grandstands, and one state-of-the-art gyro-stabilized camera is flown around the track by an expert helicopter pilot. One hundred and forty-seven microphones are placed both inside the cars and dotted around the track to pick up the noise of the cars and the crowd, with thirty timing loops embedded into the track to ensure absolute precision of lap timing.

THE PRE-WAR ERA

Ever since the days of ridden horse-drawn carts, people have wanted to race their vehicles. The practice can be dated back millennia, to the great chariot races of ancient Greece and ancient Rome. And so it should come as no surprise that no sooner had humankind invented the automobile than manufacturers and owners wanted to see how far and how fast they could make their cars go.

The first internal combustion engine is widely viewed as that designed in 1876 by the German engineer Nicolaus Otto, in which a pressurized combination of fuel and air was ignited by a spark to keep pistons turning. It was Otto's compatriot Carl Benz, however, who in 1885 created what we recognize as the first motor car, and Benz's wife, Bertha, who popularized the invention, driving great distances to publicize its reliability and usefulness.

The automobile quickly captured the world's imagination with innovative manufacturers progressing the concept at pace. The first organized car competition took place in 1894. It was a 50-mile reliability run from Paris to Rouen, France. The first contest we could call a race took place one year later, from Paris to Bordeaux and back again. Races were soon happening all over the world, and the very first Grand Prix was held in 1906, organized by the Automobile Club de France at a 65-mile-long track at Le Mans. It was won by the Hungarian driver Ferenc Szisz in a Renault. The name "Grand Prix" is the French for "big prize," and it has stuck ever since.

In the early days of car racing, drivers had to ride with a mechanic on board in case there was an issue with the car. But these long races along country roads were deemed dangerous to both competitors and the public, and so, in the first decade of the new century, permanent racing circuits were built. The very first appeared in Australia at Aspendale, in the United Kingdom at Brooklands, and in the United States at Indianapolis. In the 1920s, after a pause in racing during the First World War, more and more circuits were built around the world. In 1922, Monza, in Italy, became the first non-French host of a Grand Prix.

Two years later, the Association Internationale des Automobile Clubs Reconnus (AIACR), a forerunner of the FIA, started overseeing the running of Grands Prix. By the middle of the 1930s, nearly twenty were being held around the world, and as automobile technology increased, so did the speeds, the danger, and the esteem in which the racing drivers were held. Starting orders were determined by a ballot until the very first qualifying session took place at the 1933 Monaco Grand Prix.

For 1934, the AIACR brought in new regulations for single-driver cars: They could be no more than 750 kg (1,654 lbs), but engine size was unrestricted. By now cars were raced in national colors: blue for France, red for Italy, green for Great Britain, and white for Germany. But so marginal were the German Mercedes cars on weight that their white paint was stripped to plain metal, and thus the legend of the "Silver Arrows" was born. Together with Auto Union, which would become Audi, the German teams dominated the mid-1930s, employing the services of some of the greatest drivers of the day to take on the Italian Alfa Romeo team, run by a young Enzo Ferrari.

Drivers such as Rudolf Caracciola and Dick Seaman (Mercedes), Tazio Nuvolari (Alfa Romeo, Ferrari, and Auto Union), and Louis Chiron (Bugatti, Ferrari, and Mercedes) became legends, muscling these phenomenally fast cars with huge and powerful engines around the greatest racing circuits of the era.

But with the outbreak of the Second World War, racing was forced to stop. The bravery of a number of racing drivers was translated onto the battlefield. Some even became spies. But no sooner had hostilities ended than people demanded the return of the normality of peacetime entertainment, and as former wartime airfields became new homes for racetracks, the old cars were brought out from their slumber to resume racing. Just one year after peace was declared in Europe, the top level of global motorsport was running once again and had a brand-new name.

EVOLUTION OF CAR DESIGN

ALFA ROMEO 158
The car to beat in F1's first season

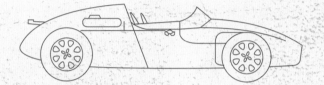

COOPER T43
The first F1 car to win a race with the engine behind the driver

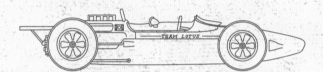

LOTUS 25
The first F1 car with a monocoque, where the engine formed a stressed part of the chassis

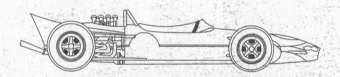

LOTUS 49B
The advent of wings in F1 for aerodynamic efficiency

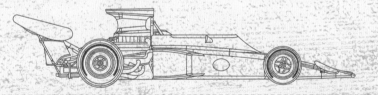

LOTUS 72
The first integrated sidepods

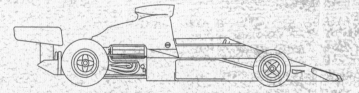

McLAREN M23
Debut of engine cover and airbox

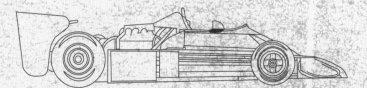

RENAULT RS01
The arrival of the turbo era

LOTUS 78
Ground effect revolution

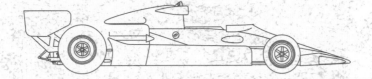

1978

McLAREN MP4/1
First car to feature a completely carbon-fiber monocoque

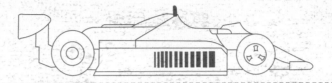

1981

WILLIAMS FW14B
Advanced electronics, driver aids, and active suspension

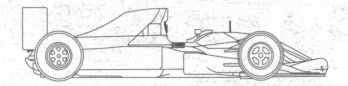

1992

FERRARI F2004
Record-breaking world championship–winning Ferrari

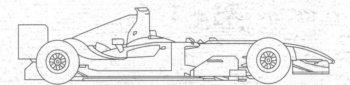

2004

McLAREN MP4/23
The peak of the battle of aerodynamics

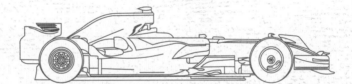

2008

BRAWN BGP001
Giant-killing car that signaled new regulations and simplified aerodynamics

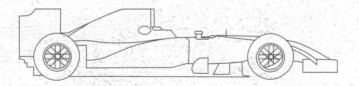

2009

MERCEDES W10
The class of the original turbo-hybrid generation

2019

RED BULL RB19
The most successful car in F1 history winning 21 of 22 Grands Prix

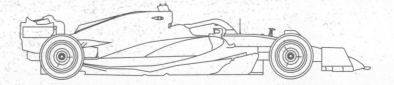

2023

EVOLUTION OF DRIVER EQUIPMENT

1950

Cloth caps

1952

Helmets are made compulsory; most popular is the Everoak Corker classic, based on polo helmets

1954

Based on fighter-pilot helmets, with a fiberglass shell and polystyrene padding, the Bell 500TX is the first helmet to pass Snell crash tests

1966

Bell Star, a full-face helmet with Nomex lining

1970S

FIA regulates construction. Medical air supply is compulsory, Nomex scarf optional

1980S-1990S

Further regulation on reduced weight, compulsory chin straps, general construction

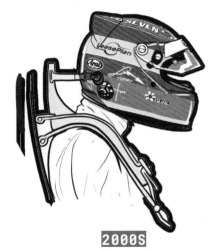

2000S

Carbon-fiber halves weigh around 1 kg (0.5 lb), and HANS is introduced

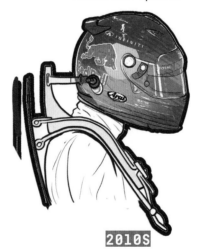

2010S

Zylon visor strip and aerodynamic wings

2020S

Narrow visor aperture, carbon-fiber and Kevlar construction

HELMETS

1950S

No regulations; civilian clothes are acceptable, but some drivers choose to wear cotton overalls

1963

FIA mandates use of fireproof overalls

1970S

The use of Nomex and Kevlar improves fire protection. Some drivers use five-layer suits built to NASA standards for astronauts.

1980S-2010S

The development of Nomex allows for suits to become lighter and thinner, while fire resistance is improved. Sponsor's embroidered patches are replaced with painted or printed decals to save weight and reduce fire risk.

OVERALLS

1950S

Large-diameter aluminum and wood, taken from road cars

1960S

Smaller leather wheels to fit enclosed cockpit

1970S

Central padding and engine kill switch

1980S

Radio talk button, suede grip, quick-release mechanism

1990S

Paddle shift and hand clutch

LATE 1990S

Carbon-fiber construction, first functionality dials

2000S

Bespoke rubber grips and move toward butterfly layout, increase in dials and buttons with over fifty settings, small digital screen

2010S

Large multi-menu screens, dials, toggles, buttons

2020S

Hundreds of variables accessible through a huge number of toggles, switches, and on screen menus

STEERING WHEELS

CIRCUIT EVOLUTION

No regulation of circuit safety, but some tracks feature hay bales as barriers

1950S

Hay bales are banned; ten-foot verges and pit walls are compulsory; guardrails, debris fences, catch fences, and sand/gravel runoff are introduced; marshal posts and service roads are mandated

1960S

FIA organizes circuit safety inspections

1970S

1980

Permanent circuit medical centers are mandated

Tire barriers are introduced and given minimum height, concrete walls replace some guardrails, and catch fencing is banned

1980S

Paved runoff and tech-pro barriers are used; tire barriers are strapped together

1990S

2000S

2010S

New tire-barrier regulations are adopted, debris shields are added to pit walls, pitlane speed limits are introduced, and curb types and heights are standardized

Improved debris fences adopt avalanche-prevention technology

THE

195

IT COULD HAVE BEEN called Formula A. The name Formula I was even suggested. But in 1946, the first set of rules for what became known as Formula 1 were agreed upon. In order to increase the number of participants and create a competitive playing field, cars with 4.5-liter, normally aspirated engines did battle against 1.5-liter supercharged racers. Large, heavy, and with engines mounted at the front, they were notoriously physical, difficult, and dangerous to drive. Nello Pagani, driving a Maserati 4CL, won the first F1 race at Pau, France, in 1947. But an organized world championship wasn't created until the next decade. The very first Formula 1 World Championship Grand Prix took place on May 13, 1950, set around the perimeter roads of a former Second World War airfield at Silverstone in England.

That first world championship consisted of seven races, six held to Formula 1 regulations and the seventh being the Indianapolis 500, the most famous and important race in America. The Indy 500 stayed on the Formula 1 calendar for the first decade of the championship's existence, even though Formula 1 drivers and teams didn't compete. However, its presence was justified in order to include a race in America and provide the impression of a true world championship. The rest of the races in that first season were all European, including those at some of the classic tracks, like Silverstone, Monaco, Spa, and Monza, which remain on the calendar today. But as Formula 1's allure and fan base grew, so too did its international appeal and race calendar. Argentina joined the championship in 1953, Morocco in 1958. The United States finally had its own Grand Prix added to the Indy 500 in 1959, in a nine-race season.

Grands Prix back then were long and arduous. Early races could run as long as 500 km (310 miles) along country roads, with little to no safety precautions. Long before safety barriers lined the tracks, hay bales and dirt banks marked the edge of the circuit and were all that existed to stop wayward racers. Cars were refueled with large metal jugs and battered funnels, and these early racing machines ran on treaded tires no wider than those you'd usually expect to see on a motorbike. Wheels were changed with the hit of a hammer against a central wheel nut. Drivers wore T-shirts and leather shoes. Helmets weren't made compulsory until 1952. Seat belts didn't exist. Danger lurked everywhere.

Points were awarded to the first five drivers across the line, and if two drivers split the driving of a car during a race, which was permitted back in the day, points were divided equally between them. To begin with, the best four results of each driver over the course of a season counted for the championship, rising to the best five and then six results as the calendar grew. In fact, points for the full season weren't counted until 1991!

To begin with, the world championship was solely a drivers' competition. The constructors' title wasn't awarded until 1958. Drivers were also free to race in other categories, and Formula 1 stars would often race in non-championship F1 events, Formula 2, Formula 3, sportscar, and IndyCar races. Many lost their lives pursuing their passion for racing, driving whatever they could, wherever they could, with any spare time they could find.

But just as today, for a driver to win, they needed an outstanding team and the fastest car. In 1950, that team was Alfa Romeo, which proved untouchable in winning every race save for the Indy 500 in the first season. In 1951, Alfa Romeo's Italian rival Ferrari swung back, taking three victories, but Alfa was again the best team, and their driver again won the championship.

Alfa Romeo withdrew from the sport in 1952, along with BRM (British Racing Motors), and with F1's entry list looking slim, the sport decided to allow Formula 2 cars to race for the next two seasons to boost entry numbers. Ferrari proved the best of the bunch, as its lead driver took back-to-back championships. But when all-new 2.5-liter atmospheric-engine Formula 1 regulations were put in place for 1954, the big teams were lured to the sport, among them Mercedes, which powered to the next two Drivers' Championships.

The 1955 season was a dark one for motorsport, however: a horrific accident at that year's 24 Hours of Le Mans resulted in hundreds of spectators injured and over eighty killed. As a result, motorsport was temporarily banned in many countries around the world. In Switzerland, all but a few motorsport events remain banned to this day. Mercedes, whose car had left the track and caused such devastation that day, withdrew from the sport—and from racing at the year's end. They wouldn't return as a team to Formula 1 until 2010.

Up against the might of the big European teams who had dominated the first years of Formula 1, small British operations had started to make their presence felt by the end of the 1950s. Their ingenuity changed the look and the technical direction of the sport forever. When the Constructors' Championship was created in 1958, it was the small British Vanwall team who won it. Technical revolution was moving at great speed, and Cooper, which had the idea to develop their fast little F3 car to run to F1 regulations, became the first manufacturer to win Grands Prix with an engine mounted not in front of the driver, but behind. By the end of the decade, Cooper were driver and team world champions. The days of the heavy front-engined cars were over. Formula 1 was moving away from its pre-war technical roots, out of postwar austerity, and into a 1960s decade that was framed by innovation and glamour—one that would, in a rapidly evolving media landscape, capture the imagination of the world.

GIUSEPPE FARINA

《 1X CHAMPION 》

Formula 1's first world champion was every bit the reflection of the upper-class roots of the sport. Giuseppe Farina was born into wealth and carried himself with the air of a man who believed he belonged at the top. Some might call that arrogance, others self-belief, but when mixed with his tremendous courage, it defined a racing style and approach that saw him make history.

"Nino," as he was known by his friends, was born in Turin, Italy's car-making heartland. His father owned an automotive bodywork shop, and his uncle Pinin founded the famous Pininfarina design company, which went on to create some of the world's most stylish cars. Pinin carried his teenage nephew as a passenger in a car race, and from there, he caught the bug. At the age of nineteen, Farina made his solo race debut—crashing out.

Nino had been sporty and academic in equal measure at school, and he was a decent soccer player, fearless skier, and a fast runner. He received a doctorate in law, joined the Italian cavalry, and served in a tank regiment. But his heart always lay in racing. In the 1930s, he was employed as a driver by Enzo Ferrari, who saw promise in his fast but accident-prone countryman. By teaming him up with the pre-war legend Tazio Nuvolari, Ferrari hoped his young charge would learn from the master. He matured into a successful driver, but the accidents that had been all too frequent from the start remained an ever-present part of his career.

Farina's driving style was brutal on his cars. He drove them hard and fast, often pushing them well beyond their mechanical limits. If he didn't crash, his cars often couldn't endure the punishment he gave them and broke down. But that mechanical brutality was hidden behind an outward calm in the driver's seat. Sitting back, arms almost fully outstretched, he appeared far more serene than many of his rivals, who hunched themselves over the wheel to wrestle their cars around the racetracks of the world.

In 1950, during Formula 1's first season, he found himself at Alfa Romeo, driving the nigh-on-unbeatable Tipo 158. The car was a carryover from racing's pre-war era, and given Alfa Romeo's knowledge of their racecar and its inherent superiority over the field, it seemed a given that one of their drivers would be the target man. Farina duly won the first Formula 1 Grand Prix in history. With subsequent wins in Switzerland and Italy, he was crowned the first-ever Formula 1 Drivers' world champion.

Farina continued racing, against his wife's wishes, until 1955, when years of accidents and injuries could no longer be tempered by the levels of morphine he'd been prescribed to numb the pain. A religious man, he believed the Virgin Mary would safeguard him in a racing car. It was to be in a road car that she lifted her protection.

In 1966, eleven years after he retired from Formula 1, the sport's first world champion died in a road accident in the Alps. He was traveling to do what he loved the most: attend a Grand Prix.

THE 1950S

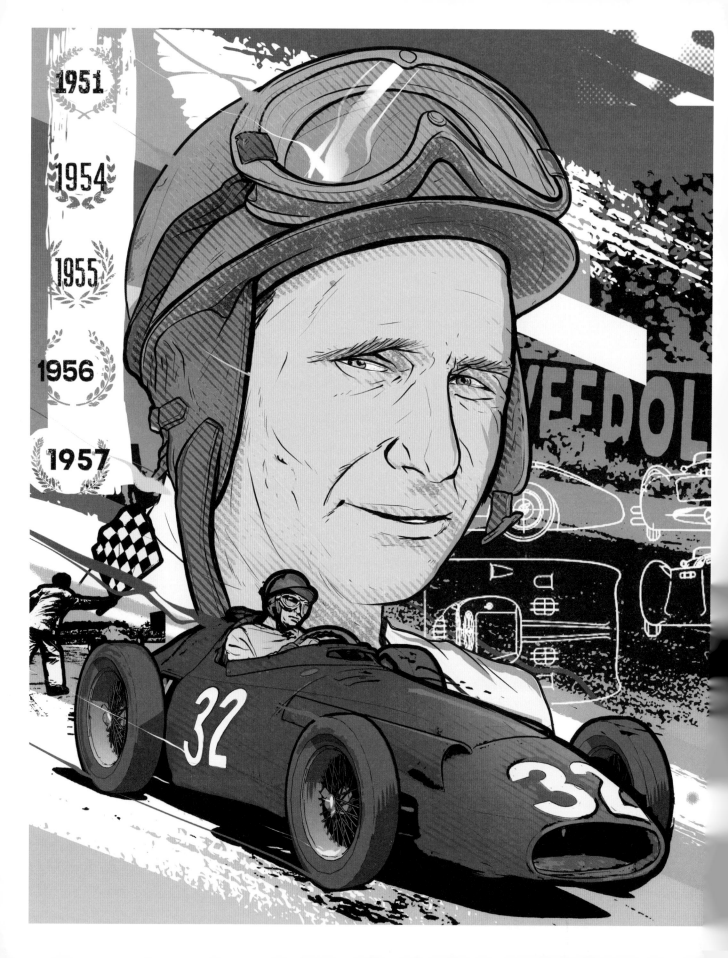

RACES 51 /// WINS 24 /// PODIUMS 35 /// POLES 29 /// FASTEST LAPS 23

JUAN MANUEL FANGIO

《 5X CHAMPION 》

If you need to know the measure of just how good Juan Manuel Fangio was, consider that Formula 1's second world champion is still regarded by many as the greatest driver who ever graced the sport. Born in the small town of Balcarce, Argentina, in 1911, he dropped out of school at the age of thirteen to pursue a career as a car mechanic. Rugged and sporty, Fangio was a keen soccer player and had offers to play professionally, but cars were his true passion.

In his twenties, Fangio opened his own garage, where he rebuilt cars that he raced in local events. They were perilous races held over many days on dirt tracks through the Argentine countryside, but his bravery and incredible natural skill saw him win races and championships. But the danger of racing caught up with him, and in 1948 he was involved in a crash that killed his co-driver. Fangio swore he would never race again.

The Argentine government, taken with Fangio's amazing ability, realized his talent would prove to be a positive international story, and after convincing him to return to racing they paid for him to travel to Europe to compete with the best in the world. When the Formula 1 World Championship began, Fangio was already almost forty years old, but his tremendous ability, stamina, physicality, and guile became legendary, and he immediately set the benchmark for those far younger than him.

Driving for Alfa Romeo, he took his first Formula 1 World Championship in 1951, but in 1952

he suffered a terrible accident in which he broke his neck. After a year of recovery, he returned in 1953 to finish second in the standings. In 1954, Fangio started the year with Maserati, but when Mercedes decided to enter the sport midseason, he jumped ship to the German manufacturer. So brilliant was the combination of Fangio and Mercedes that they won back-to-back titles in 1954 and 1955.

In 1956, Fangio moved to Ferrari after Mercedes withdrew from international competition, and again he was crowned world champion. In 1957, he returned to Maserati and, despite having to use the same car he'd raced for them at the start of 1954, was champion for a fifth time.

Fangio retired in 1958 having compiled a set of statistics that will likely never be beaten. Of the world championship races he started, he won 46 percent, was on pole position for 55 percent, and was on the podium for 67 percent. Fangio raced in sportscars, too, taking two wins at the 12 Hours of Sebring and finishing on the podium at Italy's Mille Miglia (Thousand Miles) race three times.

But Juan Manuel Fangio wasn't just a titan on the track. He was revered by his peers as the ultimate gentleman. He knew what it was to struggle and remained duly humble and gracious. His immeasurable skill, combined with his sparkling personality, made him the ultimate racer of his generation. To anyone who ever set foot in a racing car, he remains a true inspiration. He died in 1995 at the age of eighty-four as a legend.

THE 1950S

1952 WORLD CHAMPION 1953

ALBERTO ASCARI

<< 2X CHAMPION >>

Alberto Ascari was not the first driver to win a Formula 1 Grand Prix for the fabled Ferrari team, but he was their first world champion. Universally loved, respected, and revered, he was one of the safest and most dominant drivers of the early years of the sport, which made his death in a mysterious testing accident all the more heartbreaking and unfathomable.

Alberto was born into racing royalty in Milan, Italy, in 1918. His father Antonio was one of the biggest names in pre-war Grand Prix racing, and young Alberto was surrounded with the allure of speed and competition from his very first days. But he learned of racing's cruel nature early, when his father was killed at the 1925 French Grand Prix. Despite the immeasurable pain and loss, he never wavered in his desire to carry on his father's legacy.

He started his racing journey on motorbikes, but when his father's friend Enzo Ferrari invited him to compete in the 1940 Mille Miglia in one of his cars, Alberto shifted his focus to four wheels. At the end of the Second World War, Ferrari, with help from his driver Luigi Villoresi—who had become a father figure to Alberto after the death of Antonio—convinced him to keep racing. Villoresi and Ascari became team-mates at Ferrari, and in 1952, Alberto was unstoppable, winning six of seven world championship races en route to his first title. In 1953, he won a further five to secure his second. Over the course of his two championship years, he won nine consecutive championship Grand Prix victories, a record beaten only in 2023 by Max Verstappen.

Ferrari's legion of fans lovingly called Alberto "Ciccio" (Chubby), owing to his portly shape. With his light blue T-shirt pulled tight over his chest and a blue helmet sitting above his calm face while deftly handling Enzo's scarlet machines, he became the picture of Italian racing folklore. He was notoriously superstitious and wouldn't let anyone near the bag that carried his famous lucky racing kit.

He moved teams to race for Lancia from the 1954 season, and at the 1955 Monaco Grand Prix, it looked as though his luck had run out. While leading the race, Alberto lost control at the famous harbor chicane and his car launched over the barriers and into the Mediterranean Sea. Spectators feared he had sunk with his car to the ocean floor, but he floated to the surface with only bruises and a broken nose.

Days later, Alberto visited Monza, where Ferrari was testing for a race he'd entered. Alberto wasn't meant to conduct the test himself, but he insisted on running some laps to shake off the effects of his Monaco crash, despite not having his lucky race kit and helmet to hand. He never returned to the pits. At the corner that now carries his name, he crashed and perished. The reasons why were never discovered.

At the age of thirty-six, Alberto Ascari was dead, leaving the world precisely as his father Antonio had and at exactly the same age. His funeral saw one million mourners line the streets of Milan, where he was laid to rest next to his father.

THE 1950S

63

MIKE HAWTHORN

<< 1X CHAMPION >>

Mike Hawthorn was a big, bombastic character, a playboy who lived life to its fullest in every sense. Britain's first Formula 1 world champion courted controversy and column inches, demanding attention at every turn of the wheel and every twist in his personal life.

Born in 1929, Hawthorn grew up in the southern English village of Farnham, not far from the Brooklands racetrack. His father owned a garage, and Mike was immersed in the world of bikes and cars from a young age. He studied at a technical college to learn the skills to work for his father, but soon—when he wasn't terrorizing the country lanes at great speed or courting girls at local pubs—he was making a name for himself on the postwar racetracks of England.

Hawthorn made his debut in local speed trials in 1950, and his big break came just two years later at Goodwood. He won the Formula 2 race from pole position, won the Formula Libre race, and came second in the non-championship Formula 1 race all in one weekend. Mike entered the remainder of the F1 season in a private Cooper car and finished fifth in the standings. That was all Enzo Ferrari needed to see, and in 1953, Mike was racing in red. He won one race that first year, a nail-biter in which he crossed the line mere inches ahead of Juan Manuel Fangio.

Hawthorn was tall, broad, blond, and impossible to miss. He was the veritable life and soul of every party, with a distinct style and class. This translated to his racing attire, where he famously wore a bow tie over his racing overalls. But his notoriety gave rise to scandal. His relationships with leading ladies of the day were headline news. He was even accused in parliament of dodging military service; the truth was that he was denied entry to the armed forces on account of a debilitating and incurable kidney disease. Mike was brave. He survived horrific burns in a non-championship race in Sicily in 1954, and he continued to race through the pain.

Hawthorn was no stranger to controversy on the track, either. In 1955, he was blamed by many for causing a crash between Lance Macklin and Pierre Levegh at the 24 Hours of Le Mans. This tragedy resulted in the deaths of eighty-four people and saw motorsport banned in a number of countries, while Mercedes withdrew from racing altogether.

After moving teams multiple times in Formula 1 and enjoying a fantastic rivalry with fellow Brit Sir Stirling Moss, Mike found himself back at Ferrari in 1957, where he built one of the most profound relationships of his life with his teammate Peter Collins. They became inseparable, more like brothers than colleagues.

Hawthorn won the world championship in 1958 by a single point over Moss, but his love for racing was already gone due to Collins' death at the Nürburgring earlier in the year. He retired as soon as the season was over, and was killed in a road accident just months later. At the time of his death, Hawthorn's kidney disease was so advanced that reports say he had just eighteen months left to live.

1959
1960
1966

SIR JACK
BRABHAM

《 3X CHAMPION 》

Sir Jack Brabham holds a record that will likely never be repeated in Formula 1 history: he is the only man to have ever won a world championship while driving for his own team. As adept at perfecting setups as he was talented behind the wheel, he was a shrewd businessman with one eye always on the future. Few in the history of the sport have had as lasting an impact or influenced the very fabric of the sport as deeply.

Born in 1926 in Hurstville, near Sydney, Australia, Jack learned to drive delivery vehicles for his father's grocery business years before he was eligible for a license, though his main job was making sure they ran. At fifteen, he left school to work in a garage, and at eighteen he joined the Australian Air Force, where he served as a mechanic during the Second World War. In 1950s peacetime, Jack was convinced by a friend to start racing midgets, small front-engined cars that race on dirt ovals. Jack prepared his own cars and won multiple championships and hillclimbs before shifting his focus to road racing with a move to England.

There he met the owners of the Cooper car company, and Jack convinced them to move their revolutionary rear-engined cars into Formula 1. The move was inspired, and although Sir Stirling Moss took the first rear-engined F1 victory with a privately entered Cooper in 1958, Jack became the last world champion of the 1950s with a brilliant display in the factory Cooper in 1959.

Jack followed it up in 1960 with back-to-back titles after completely dominating the season, as Cooper's rivals hadn't yet realized the genius in the new car design philosophy. By 1961, Cooper was overtaken by far richer rivals, and so in 1962, Jack started his own team. Recruiting the brilliant American Dan Gurney to race alongside him, Brabham's team finished third in the 1963 season. In 1966, engine regulations changed, and Jack again used his genius to work with the Australian company Repco to amend an old engine to the new rules. As other engines failed, the reliability of Jack's gave him his third championship, and his first with his own team.

As the years went by, Jack tried repeatedly to retire. But at seemingly every turn, his lead driver was poached by someone else, and so he'd stay on until someone better could be found. As more of his friends perished in the unrelenting dangers of the sport in the 1960s, Jack grew weary. He finally called it a day at the end of the 1970 F1 season, but not before one final victory at the South African Grand Prix at age forty-four. The quiet man who never lost the racing flair he'd learned on the dirt tracks of his youth retired and eventually sold his team. He watched his sons embark on their own racing careers, and in 1985, he was knighted by Queen Elizabeth II for services to British motorsport. He lived out the rest of his life in peace at home in Australia until his death in 2014 at the age of eighty-eight.

THE 1950S

SIR STIRLING
MOSS

Sir Stirling Moss is widely regarded as the finest driver never to win the Formula 1 World Championship. Blisteringly quick in any and every car he jumped into, he was the consummate all-rounder, venerated by rivals and loved by all.

Stirling was born into a racing family in 1929. His childhood was privileged but tough, and he was bullied at school for his Jewish heritage, something that he later admitted gave him a fire to succeed. He passed his driving test at fifteen, and four years later, he began a racing career that would make him a global icon. He raced anything, anywhere: Formula 1, sportscars, touring cars, speed records, rallying. You name it, he raced it, and chances were, he won. At one point in his career he ran sixty-two races in a single year.

Formula 1 was always his goal, and the big players were quick to notice his talent. Moss began his F1 journey in a privately entered Maserati, and although the car was unreliable, Moss often found himself racing against the best. At the 1954 Italian Grand Prix, he was on for the win until his engine gave up. He got out and pushed his car to the finish line. Alfred Neubauer, the team boss of Mercedes, had seen enough and signed him for the next season.

Moss lined up for Mercedes in 1955 alongside Juan Manuel Fangio, and together they formed an unstoppable force in both Formula 1 and sportscars. He won the Mille Miglia, finishing in ten hours at an average speed of 100 mph, in what is often considered the greatest drive in history.

When Mercedes withdrew from motorsport and Moss believed Ferrari had messed him around over a potential seat, he decided he'd only ever compete for British teams again, racing for Vanwall and then for Rob Walker's private team. He finished second in the world championship four times and third three times. In 1958, Moss was denied the championship by a single point only because he refused to allow the race stewards to give compatriot Mike Hawthorn a penalty in the year's final race. His honor and integrity meant more to him than the crown.

Stirling Moss rarely crashed, but he was involved in a huge accident at Goodwood in 1962. He fell into a coma for a month, and when he emerged, he realized swiftly that his racing reactions were gone. His racing career was over, but a career in broadcasting stood before him, and so he was never far from a racetrack. He often popped up in one-off races, just for a bit of fun, and he was a regular on the historic tours. Moss only officially announced his retirement in 2011 at the age of eighty-one.

In total, Moss officially entered 529 circuit races in his fifteen-year professional career and won 212 of them, figures that don't even include his many speed trials, rallies, record attempts, and hillclimbs. To many, Stirling Moss *was* motor racing—the definition of sporting bravery and gentlemanly decency. He passed away peacefully in 2020 at the age of ninety.

THE 1950S

JOSÉ FROILÁN GONZÁLES

Like Juan Manuel Fangio, José Froilán Gonzáles came to Europe with the backing of the Argentine government, and while the two were genuine rivals on track, they had a shared satisfaction in each other's successes. "Pepe," as he was known, had another nickname, "the Pampas Bull," which was indicative of his red rag approach to Grand Prix racing. He was flat out 100 percent of the time—on track, on dirt and grass, he seemed never to lift off. His huge frame hustled his cars, and his finest day came at the 1951 British Grand Prix, where he defied the odds to beat the Alfa Romeos and take Ferrari's first Formula 1 win.

PETER COLLINS

Good-looking and carefree, Peter Collins was lightning behind the wheel. Although not the most technically minded, he could extract pretty much everything that a car could give. His attitude and speed garnered the attention of Enzo Ferrari, who signed him for 1956. After the death of his son, the distraught Enzo treated Peter like a member of the family. Collins rewarded Enzo's love with consistent results. He formed an incredible partnership with Mike Hawthorn, the two becoming like brothers, living life to the fullest on and off track. Tragically, he was killed at the 1958 German Grand Prix, pushing to the limit, the only way he knew to race.

TONY BROOKS

In an era of big, heavy cars and big, physical racing drivers, Tony Brooks was the exception. Slim and slight in build, he was a picture of calm serenity behind the wheel, one of the first Formula 1 drivers who could be said to have driven a car with his fingertips. Yet despite his alternative style, he was rapid. A multiple Grand Prix winner, he finished third and second in the world championship and was admired throughout the paddock as a brilliant racer and a true gentleman. Crashes in sportscars made him pledge never again to race cars in less than perfect conditions, and he retired from the sport in 1961.

MARIA TERESA DE FILIPPIS

The first woman to race in Formula 1, Maria Teresa de Filippis was a trailblazer. She made a name for herself in sportscars, coming second in the 1954 Italian sportscar championship and finishing second in a sportscar race supporting the 1956 Naples Grand Prix. She qualified for three championship Grands Prix with a best result of tenth in the 1958 Belgian Grand Prix and fifth at the non-championship Syracuse Grand Prix. Her bravery won her the admiration of her fellow male competitors, with the legendary Juan Manuel Fangio and Stirling Moss left in no doubt as to her speed.

TITANS OF THE 1950s

ALFA ROMEO

Had the Constructors' World Championship existed when Formula 1 began, Alfa Romeo would have been utterly dominant: their cars won all but three Grands Prix in 1950 and 1951. What is perhaps even more astonishing is that the team's all-conquering cars—the Alfetta 158 and its development into the 159, which it ran in 1950 and 1951—were essentially the exact same car the team had run in the late 1930s. The 158 already had eighteen victories under its belt by the time the Formula 1 World Championship had even begun. Being such a known quantity made it a reliable and sensible option for the first years of the championship, and it was relatively cheap to run. But as costs rose, Alfa Romeo's request for government assistance to continue racing came to naught, and at the end of 1951, they were forced to withdraw from the sport.

FERRARI

Scuderia Ferrari is the only team to have competed in every Grand Prix season since the inception of the sport in 1950. When Enzo Ferrari founded his team in 1929, the idea of building his own cars was a distant dream. He began by running Alfa Romeos, and he was so successful that his team effectively became the official factory Alfa Romeo outfit from 1933 to the outbreak of the Second World War. By the time the Formula 1 World Championship began, over two decades after he'd started his team, Enzo had his own factory and was building his own road and race cars. His Ferrari 375 held a whopping 4.5-liter, V12 engine, which took his drivers to their first F1 victories in 1951. With new regulations for 1952, Ferrari was the only team that had adequately prepared, and its beautiful Ferrari 500 swept to back-to-back titles, winning fourteen championship Grands Prix in a row. Regardless of the nearly annual regulation changes, Ferrari persisted and remained consistently competitive in the first decade of Formula 1. It won races in every season save for 1950 and 1957, and its drivers took four championships and twenty-seven race wins, almost exactly a third of all Grands Prix contested in the sport's first decade.

VANWALL

Vanwall

Founded by the British industrialist Tony Vandervell, Vanwall had a short but illustrious tenure in Formula 1: Vanwall was the first British team to win a Formula 1 Grand Prix and was the very first team to win the Constructors' World Championship. The first Vanwalls raced in 1954, but it wasn't until 1956 and 1957 that the team saw success. Vandervell had employed the services of the promising young designer Colin Chapman and the aerodynamicist Frank Costin, who together had created the VW5. It took its first win at the 1957 British Grand Prix, and in 1958, it proved to be the class of the field, winning six F1 races at the hands of Sir Stirling Moss and Tony Brooks to seal that very first constructors' title. With Vandervell's health failing, the team withdrew from full-time competition in 1959 and from racing altogether in 1961.

COOPER

The Cooper Car Company began making racing cars in the late 1940s and pioneered the idea of moving the engine from in front of to behind the driver, a concept that improved the balance and agility of racing cars and forever changed the face of Formula 1. Initially, the idea was born of necessity, as Cooper's popular 500cc F3 cars used motorcycle engines, meaning the chain had to be close to the rear axle. Their rapid little race cars became so successful that they were heavily in demand. But it was only in the mid-1950s, when Cooper developed a sportscar with an engine behind the driver, that it suddenly realized what it could achieve if it took its revolutionary idea to Formula 1. In 1957, Sir Jack Brabham took one of these mid-engined Cooper F1 cars to points in Monaco. In 1958, Sir Stirling Moss won the Argentine Grand Prix in a privately entered Cooper. And in 1959, Brabham was world champion, driving for Cooper, whose team was crowned the Constructors' World Champion. And all with their revolutionary idea of putting the engine behind the driver. No front-engined car would ever win a Formula 1 World Championship again.

MASERATI

Think of Formula 1 in the 1950s, and you can't help but think of Maserati. The 250F, which the team launched in 1954, became one of the most popular and widely used in the sport for the remainder of the decade, launching careers and becoming a favorite of private entrants even once front-engined cars began to become obsolete. The 250F took Juan Manuel Fangio to two wins at the start of the 1954 season before he defected to Mercedes; then it brought him to four victories on his return to the team in 1957 and to his final world title that year.

MERCEDES

The Silver Arrows of Mercedes appeared in just twelve Grands Prix in 1954 and 1955, but in that time, they took seventeen podiums and nine victories, and helped Juan Manuel Fangio to two titles. Arriving midseason in 1954, their W196 used direct fuel-injection, developed from German Luftwaffe technology used by the Messerschmitt fighter planes during the Second World War. The car had two body designs—one open wheel and another streamlined for the faster races like Monza—and both proved almost unbeatable. The W196 influenced the Mercedes 300 SLR, which raced at Le Mans and was at the center of the 1955 tragedy that forced Mercedes to withdraw from competition. The team would not return to Formula 1 as a constructor until 2010.

THE 1950S

RACE OF THE DECADE

1957 GERMAN GRAND PRIX

It should probably come as little surprise that, as the driver who defined the decade, Juan Manuel Fangio's greatest race is often regarded as the finest of the era. And it's not just viewed that way by fans or pundits—the great man himself believed that the 1957 German Grand Prix was the best Formula 1 performance of his life.

The Nürburgring was a terrifying circuit in its original form. At 22 km (13.7 miles), with over 160 corners, it was a circuit hewn from nature, scything its way through the Eifel mountains, notorious for terrible weather and danger lurking around every corner: the "Green Hell," as it would come to be known.

Fangio had won at the infamous track before—twice in fact. But in 1957, at the wheel of the aging Maserati 250F, he felt he didn't have a chance against the Ferraris. Although Fangio had the edge over a lap, he and Maserati were aware that Ferrari had better race pace and would defeat him over the full distance, all things being equal. He determined that if he was to have any chance of the win, he would have to run with his fuel tanks half full and absolutely rip through his tires, stopping at half distance of the twenty-two-lap race to top up on fuel, take on new tires, and go again.

As the race began, Fangio, in a light car only half full of fuel, set about pulling a gap to the Ferraris and by half distance was half a minute ahead; that was ample time to make his stop and emerge in the lead. But a delay in the pits meant that, when he emerged back into the race, he found himself around fifty seconds behind the leading cars of the Scuderia with only ten laps remaining. It looked for all the world as though there was no hope. And yet, this was Fangio. He set off after the leaders, breaking lap record after lap record, taking risks he had never taken, driving corners faster and in higher gears than he had ever thought possible. He didn't so much chip away at the lead as take almighty chunks out of it lap after lap. Fangio found himself in a state of racing perfection he had never experienced before.

With two laps to go, he first caught sight of Peter Collins and then Mike Hawthorn in their scarlet Ferraris. He reeled them both in, passed them, and took the lead. Even his seat breaking on the very final lap couldn't slow him down—he clung onto the wheel to hold himself up, while still powering around the most difficult and dangerous circuit ever raced in Formula 1.

He won by three seconds and was visibly emotional as he took to the podium. He didn't sleep for two days afterward, as the enormity of what he'd done took hold of him. His fastest race lap was more than eight seconds faster than the one with which he'd taken pole position. It was his finest race, his bravest drive, and his final victory in Formula 1, handing him an astonishing fifth world championship.

THE

196

THE 1960S BEGAN AS the 1950s had ended, with Formula 1 teams facing the key decision of whether to stick with their old ways or follow the revolutionary lead of the new British outfits. While Enzo Ferrari had always insisted carts were pulled by horses, not pushed, the tide had turned against front-engined cars and never again would world championships be won by the old designs.

Cooper picked up where they'd left off, winning the titles again in 1960, but in 1961, an engine regulation change came at the right time for Ferrari. The shift in rules to 1.5-liter, normally aspirated engines (or force induced at half that capacity) allowed the great Italian team the freedom to take the new path, building their first rear-engined car and a hugely powerful engine. In so doing, they created one of the most memorable and beautiful cars in F1 history, the Sharknose 156.

British teams scrambled to catch up. They were derided as "garagistes" by the European "grandees" for running their simple race operations from garages rather than grand factories, which created road cars alongside racers. Long before regulations determined that teams had to be constructors in their own right, the freedom of the Brits lay in either designing their own chassis or buying one off the shelf and simply bolting on the best engine and transmissions

they could find. For the majority of the 1960s, that engine was the Coventry Climax V8. Former Vanwall designer Colin Chapman had by now started his own team, Lotus, an outfit that became the byword for invention and innovation in the sport. Soon they were the team to beat.

Yet another engine formula change occurred in 1966 when the capacity was doubled to 3.0 liters for normally aspirated engines or 1.5 liters for super or turbocharged units. Incredibly, Coventry Climax withdrew rather than adapt their 1.5-liter engines, leaving the field open for the revolutionary Ford Cosworth DFV, which would become the go-to engine of choice for independent F1 teams for the next decade.

But it wasn't just the power delivery that was changing. The DFV allowed designers to bolt an engine directly onto a chassis at the rear of the cockpit, rather than drop an engine inside a longer tubular chassis. This design choice—making the engine a stressed part of the car rather than a part that was added in—has affected every F1 car made since.

Aerodynamics were, by now, also becoming an increasingly key differential to a car's performance, and by the late 1960s, Formula 1 cars had started to sprout wings. Lotus began the trend in 1968, and before long these appendages had grown in size, multiplied in placement, and become more sophisticated as designers understood their power and potential for speed. They proved unreliable on occasion, however, and major accidents at the 1969 Spanish Grand Prix led to an immediate ban on wing use. But later in the season, they were reinstated at a much reduced size and only permitted at regulated positions.

With an increase in technology and speed came an increase in danger. Fourteen drivers lost their lives at the wheel of Formula 1 machinery in the 1960s, with many others perishing while racing elsewhere. For many, the death of multiple F1 champion Jim Clark in a Formula 2 race proved to be a pivotal moment—for if the racer considered by all to be the greatest of his day could be lost, what chance did any of them have of making it out alive?

Sir Jackie Stewart became a vocal advocate for safety, organizing driver boycotts and pushing circuit owners to step up and safeguard the racers risking their lives on the track. Dan Gurney became the first driver to use a full-face helmet in Formula 1 in 1968, and soon after they became the norm.

The reach of the world championships grew further, with the now-shorter Grands Prix of 300 km (186 miles) held at new destinations in South Africa, Mexico, and Canada. Plus, a regular US Grand Prix replaced the Indy 500 alongside an ever-growing calendar in Europe. Greater public interest was drawn from increasingly widespread television ownership and coverage, as Formula 1 highlights appeared on nightly news and dedicated sports roundups, and the champions of the day became popular guests on variety and celebrity interview shows.

Even the silver screen came calling, as John Frankenheimer directed *Grand Prix*, a 1966 Hollywood epic that was filmed during an entire season of the Formula 1 World Championship and featured many of the drivers of the day. The film went on to win three Academy Awards and is still widely regarded as one of the best racing films ever made.

From The Beatles to Grace Kelly, celebrities started to show up at Grands Prix as guests and fascinated spectators. As the allure of the sport permeated the social zeitgeist, major corporations wanted a part of the action. In 1968, the FIA allowed unrestricted sponsorship for the first time, and teams were quick to pick up on the opportunity, ditching their national colors for those of their backers.

Formula 1, its teams, and its new generation of superstar drivers were now marketable assets, whose stars shone on track, on screen, and in media coverage around the world. Formula 1 was going global, but its ascent into the popular consciousness had only just begun.

PHIL HILL

《 1X CHAMPION 》

Formula 1 tried for seventy years to establish itself in the United States. Yet America had an F1 champion at the start of its second decade, and what's more, one who raced for the sport's most famous team—Ferrari. A man of paradox, Phil Hill drove with great courage and tremendous speed, and yet he was overcome with debilitating nerves and anxiety over the immense dangers inherent in the sport he conquered.

Incredibly intelligent and considerate, Hill made few friends in his youth, developing a feeling of inadequacy throughout a childhood in which he wanted for nothing from his rich parents. His love for the automotive world developed at an early age when a beloved aunt bought him a car that he took apart and rebuilt countless times to learn how it worked. He dropped out of college to become a mechanic, and his intrigue with all things automotive led him to buy, modify, and eventually race his own cars. When his parents died and left him a vast fortune, he bought his first Ferrari, in which he raced and won.

By the mid-1950s, he was the go-to racer of choice for American sportscar owners, and he won the 24 Hours of Le Mans an incredible three times. Enzo Ferrari recognized his talents but believed him a sportscar specialist. But in 1958, following the deaths of both Luigi Musso and Peter Collins, Ferrari turned to Hill to pilot one of his Formula 1 cars. With two podiums in the final two races of 1958, Hill helped Ferrari team-mate Mike Hawthorn win the title. And with that, Hill's place at the top of the sport was secured.

Although he drove outdated front-engined Ferraris for the next two years, he still impressed, winning his first Grand Prix at Monza in 1960. Then in 1961, when Ferrari delivered their famous, rapid rear-engined Sharknose 156, he was able to fight for the world championship.

The specter of death always troubled Hill. He made his first Le Mans start at that fateful 1955 race, and he was only granted his spot on the Ferrari F1 team due to the deaths of the team's Grand Prix stars of the day. He would smoke on the grid, pacing up and down trying to cope with the emotional turmoil of the risks he was about to take, but once the races began, he became a picture of calm and successfully mastered some of the world's most dangerous circuits.

He and team-mate Wolfgang von Trips proved the class of the field in 1961, but when Hill's victory in the Italian Grand Prix, the final race of the season, assured him the title, there was no celebration from the new world champion. Von Trips had been killed in the race, his crash taking innocent spectators with him.

Disillusioned with the sport and torn over the tragedy through which his title had been won, Hill retired from Formula 1 in 1964, though he continued to race in sportscars until the end of 1967. He moved back to California, married his girlfriend, started a family, and set up a car restoration company. Many say there has never been a more intelligent or contemplative world champion than Phil Hill. He died at age eighty-one in 2008.

THE 1960S

1962
1968

GRAHAM HILL

《 2X CHAMPION 》

Graham Hill was the first true star of Grand Prix racing. With a slicked-back hairdo and mustachioed top lip, he was dashing and debonair, with a wit as quick as his racecraft. While the first two world champions of the 1960s shared a surname, they could not have been more different characters or have hailed from more different backgrounds.

Hill was born in 1929 and grew up in war-torn London, where rationing and bombing by the German Luftwaffe were a part of everyday life. He endured military service in the Royal Navy, which he hated, but he retained a love for water through the London Rowing Club, of which he was a member. He would later carry the club's insignia of white blades on a navy background on his racing helmet.

A chance opportunity in 1953 saw him try to drive a Formula 3 car, something that he immediately loved. The only issue was that Graham Hill had never learned to drive, and so the determined Englishman made the decision to both gain a license and find enough money to race.

He spent his unemployment benefit on his hobby, and he eventually found a part-time job working as a mechanic for Colin Chapman at Lotus. As reward for his hard work, he was given an occasional chance to race by his new boss, who was immediately impressed by what he saw.

When Lotus entered Formula 1 in the late 1950s, Hill was chosen as one of its drivers. But after two years of little success, Hill sought new opportunities with BRM. He found a team in the doldrums, but with talismanic leadership qualities, Hill motivated the squad to renewed success and, in 1962, the Formula 1 World Championship.

Charming, affable, and a veritable riot outside the car, Hill was no party boy when it came to the seriousness of his on-track career. He raced hard and was diligent in the application of his talents. He had a clear idea of changes he wanted made to his cars and had a short temper for those who didn't toe the line. He returned to Lotus in 1967 and summoned all of his leadership skills to take the team to the title in 1968 following the death of their lead driver, Jim Clark.

Now a two-time champion, Hill was a force everywhere, but nowhere more than in Monte Carlo. With five wins at the classic track, he was fittingly dubbed "Mr. Monaco." But it wasn't just Formula 1 in which Hill excelled. He won the Indy 500 and the 24 Hours of Le Mans, making him the only man in history—to this day—to complete the fabled Triple Crown of Motorsport.

By the 1970s, Hill had established his own racing team, but after failing to qualify for Monaco in 1975, he called it a day and hung up his helmet. Returning home from a test in France later that year, Hill, piloting his team's twin-engine plane, crashed in heavy fog near London. All on board were killed. His death left a nation, and a family, in mourning, none more than his teenage son, Damon.

THE 1960S

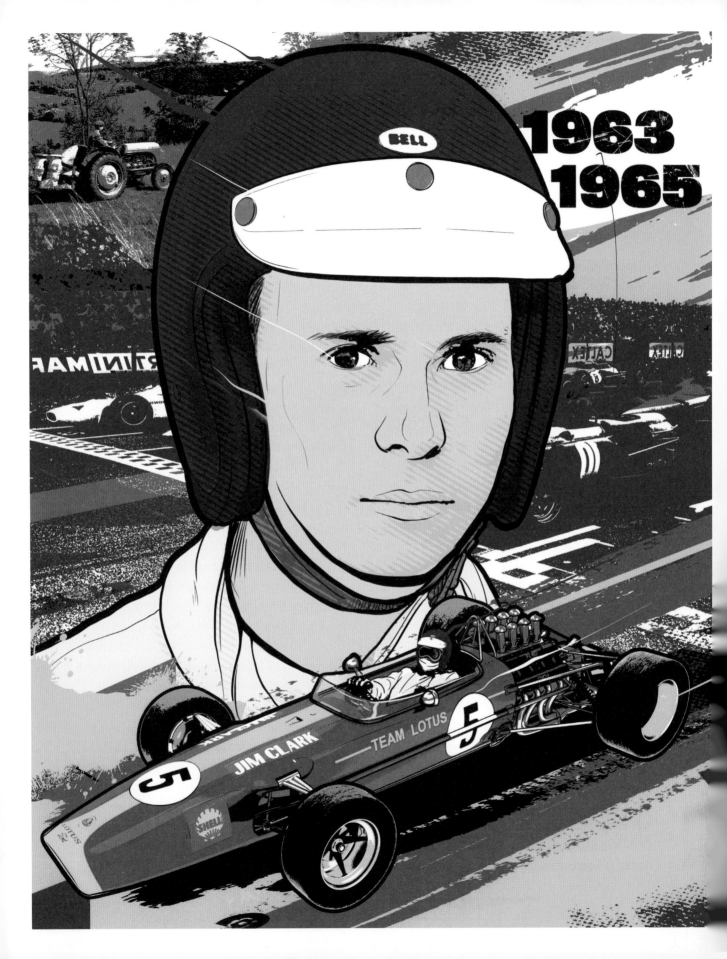

JIM CLARK

《 2X CHAMPION 》

The argument over who is truly the greatest driver in Formula 1 history will perhaps never be settled. There are simply too many variables to make any comparison meaningful. Yet whenever lists are compiled, one name usually finds its way close to the top. Because Jim Clark wasn't just good or even great. He was exceptional.

Born in 1936, Clark grew up on his family's sheep farm in Scotland. From an early age, he could be found pushing a tractor to its limits in the fields, and when he turned seventeen, the very first thing he did was get a driver's license. He started his racing career in secret, but that quickly became impossible. Winning came with such apparent ease that he progressed from his earliest small local races in 1956 to his Formula 1 debut in 1960.

He spent his entire F1 career racing for Lotus, which proved both a blessing and a curse. While Colin Chapman's cars were always at the forefront of technical ingenuity, they were also fragile and unreliable. Clark could and arguably should have been champion in 1962, but an oil leak in the season's final race stopped him. He lost the title in exactly the same way in 1964. But in 1963 and 1965, his Lotus held together, and he was unstoppable, winning two well-deserved world championships.

Although 1966 proved to be a frustrating season with an uncompetitive car, Clark's relationship with Chapman was almost brotherly. The charming, shy Scotsman had absolute belief in his friend, and

by 1967, they were back at the front again. In total they won twenty-five races together, a record at the time. In 1965, they won the Indy 500 together, too. An F1 world champion, Indy 500 winner, Tasman Series champion, French F2 champion, and winner of a bunch of saloon car races, Clark was simply supreme.

Like Sir Stirling Moss, Jim Clark was fast in anything and everything, and like Moss, Clark didn't make mistakes. He drove as if in the middle of a beautiful ballet—effortless, seemingly choreographed perfection. If he didn't win, chances were it was because the car let him down and he failed to see the flag.

After winning the opening Grand Prix of 1968, he entered a Formula 2 race at Hockenheim in Germany. In dreadful conditions, his car left the track on the fifth lap and slammed into the trees. In an instant, Jim Clark was gone. While no definitive cause was established, the most likely explanation was a deflating rear tire. His death hit the world of motorsport hard. He was considered, even among his tremendously talented peers, to be the very best there was.

He was laid to rest near his family's farm in Scotland, the title on his headstone reflecting the humble nature of the man. It simply reads "FARMER" before briefly listing his motorsport successes. To anyone who ever saw him race, and to legions of fans who were never granted that pleasure, he remains the single greatest driver who ever lived.

THE 1960S

85

JOHN SURTEES

« 1X CHAMPION »

The only man to win world championships on both two and four wheels, John Surtees was as much a force to be reckoned with on track as he was off track, his fearless drive and determination being the traits that both laid the foundations for his incredible success in motorsport and created political hurdles he struggled to negotiate.

Surtees was born into a racing family in London in 1934. His father was a motorcycle side-car champion, and before he'd even reached his teens, John was riding bikes of his own. He started racing at sixteen, won his first race at seventeen, and by the mid-1950 was part of the Norton factory team, winning sixty-eight of his seventy-six races. Between 1956 and 1960, he rode for the Italian MV Agusta outfit, winning seven championships, and the Isle of Man TT six times in the 350cc and 500cc classes. In 1958 and 1959, he won every race he entered.

His bravery and brilliance were unquestionable, and he could easily have continued racing bikes had he wished. But he wanted a new challenge and transitioned to four wheels with immediate success. In his first Formula 3 race in 1960, he ran home second to Jim Clark. He was granted an immediate F1 debut, but although he took some podiums, the stars didn't align until he moved to the biggest name in the sport. In 1963, his first year at Ferrari, he retired from more races than he finished, but of the four results that stood, he finished fourth, third, second, and finally first at the Nürburgring in Germany, reflecting the

promise in the partnership. It all came together for Ferrari and Surtees in 1964, as he swept to six podiums, bringing him the world championship and a unique place in history.

He won once more for Ferrari, at Belgium in 1966 in one of his greatest drives, but after a huge political fallout with top management, he sensationally quit the sport's most famous team midseason. His forthright nature made him a tough man to deal with, and the sensibilities and eggshell-walking required in Formula 1 were never Surtees' strength. He was simply too blunt and truthful to play the game, having cut his teeth in the simpler, less precious world of bikes.

He won just twice more in F1, once for Cooper in 1966 and once for Honda in 1967. He saw the podium again only twice after that, despite carrying on in the sport for five more years, eventually running his own team starting in 1970. He retired at the end of 1972 to focus on the squad that carried his name, but eventually, medical problems brought about by a huge crash in 1965 proved too much, and he closed the doors on the Surtees squad in 1978.

In retirement he focused on his health, and his fierce side calmed considerably. He aged into a mellow and much-loved member of the paddock. He married three times and had three children. He spent his later years dedicated to the foundation he set up in memory of his son, Henry, who was killed in a Formula 2 race in 2009. John Surtees passed away in 2017 at age eighty-three.

THE 1960S

87

DENNY HULME

« 1X CHAMPION »

Denny Hulme is often considered the forgotten world champion. To some he appeared unfriendly and brusque, but that was due mainly to the short shrift he gave those who hadn't appreciated his skills before he won the greatest prize in motorsport. In truth, he was a modest man who never cared much for celebrity and was embarrassed by it. He hated public appearances. He did his talking on the track, and in his prime he was mighty, respected by everyone he raced, particularly those whose names have become far more readily remembered.

Born in New Zealand in 1936, Hulme was driving his father's trucks by the age of six. Like many of his generation, he became a mechanic and a truck driver who dreamed of one day emulating his European heroes, the drivers he'd heard stories about from their time racing in the Australasian Tasman Series. He showed promise in local races, and in 1959 he won a scholarship to race abroad. His skills came to the attention of Sir Jack Brabham, for whom he worked as a mechanic, and in 1963, Hulme won seven Formula Junior races. The next season he helped his boss to win the Formula 2 title, and in 1965 and 1966, he joined Brabham in Formula 1.

Hulme's year was 1967, when he was crowned world champion after magnificent wins at both Monaco and the Nürburgring, as well as six other podiums. His curt reputation was cemented when he rebuked and ignored those who had given him little positive press before he became

champion. The Johnny-come-latelies simply didn't deserve his time or his effort.

In 1968, he joined compatriot Bruce McLaren's team and never raced in Formula 1 for anyone else again, even after McLaren's death in 1970. Hulme won six Grands Prix in McLaren machinery and two Can-Am (Canadian-American Challenge Cup) titles for the team. He took a class win at Le Mans and was Ken Miles' co-driver at Ford for the 1966 24 Hours of Le Mans, where they believed they'd won the whole thing, only to be classified second—a story now immortalized in the film *Ford v Ferrari*.

He retired from racing at the end of 1974 after the harrowing death of his friend Peter Revson on the track—it was an emotional hurdle he couldn't overcome. He returned to New Zealand having lost too many friends, along with having his own injuries to contend with.

But the racer in him lived on, and he continued to compete in historic races alongside regular appearances at one of his favorite events, Australia's famous Bathurst 1,000-km (621-mile) touring car race.

In 1992, eighteen years after his Formula 1 retirement, his car pulled to the side of the Bathurst track and stopped. The 1967 world champion had suffered a heart attack and died doing what he treasured and what he was so very good at—giving his all, behind the wheel, on a racetrack he loved.

THE 1960S

89

SIR JACKIE STEWART

« 3X CHAMPION »

Sir Jackie Stewart's childhood was not a happy one. Mocked and bullied at school, he struggled academically and was given little hope by his teachers for a life that had anything to offer other than disappointment. Yet despite such a difficult beginning, his story would see him become a Knight of the Realm, a three-time Formula 1 World Champion, a team owner, and one of the most influential racers in the history of the sport, his drive to make F1 safer changing motor racing and improving road safety around the world.

Born in Scotland in 1939, Stewart had dyslexia, which went undiagnosed and was misunderstood. Unable to read or write, he left school at fifteen to work at his father's garage. There he discovered that he was incredibly coordinated and good with his hands, which developed his confidence to try his hand at clay shooting, in which he excelled.

Stewart's work with cars, however, had also led him to attempt racing, and he showed immediate potential, catching the attention of Ken Tyrrell, who signed him to race in Formula 3. He won seven races in 1964 and was crowned the F3 champion. From there, Stewart had his pick of Formula 1 teams. He opted to turn down the advances of Lotus to race instead for BRM, feeling he stood a better chance of standing out against Graham Hill than he would being classified as a number two to Jim Clark.

His assuredness and thoughtfulness proved prescient, and he took his first win that year at Monza. In 1968, he signed for Matra, reuniting with Ken Tyrrell as team boss and finishing second in the championship with three wins. The very next year, he took six victories and was named world champion.

In 1970, Tyrrell set up his own team, and the ever-loyal Stewart raced for Ken for the rest of his career, taking sixteen further wins and two world championships in 1971 and 1973. He withdrew before the start of what would have been his one-hundredth and final race after witnessing the horrific death of his team-mate and dear friend François Cevert. Stewart had lived with the specter of death throughout his career, and after many accidents of his own and the loss of many friends like Cevert, he advocated for improved safety in the sport. He was often a lone voice in his dedication to safety and became deeply unpopular in some quarters, as he led race boycotts until tracks were changed or medical facilities improved.

In retirement Stewart became a popular television pundit and commentator, and in 1997 he returned to Formula 1 as a team owner, with his son Paul. With funding from Ford, they launched Stewart Grand Prix, which competed for three years and took a race win in the 1999 European Grand Prix. Ford bought the team and changed its name to Jaguar in 2000 before selling it to drinks magnate Dietrich Mateschitz to form Red Bull Racing.

Sir Jackie Stewart attends Grands Prix to this day as a legend of the sport. He continues to advocate for race safety, alongside tireless work for his charity Race Against Dementia, which he established to help find a cure for the disease that has afflicted his wife and childhood sweetheart, Helen.

THE 1960S

91

DAN GURNEY

Dan Gurney may have won just four Grands Prix in his career and finished only as high as fourth in a Formula 1 season, but he is widely regarded as one of the greatest Americans to ever set foot in a racing car and one of the most gifted and fastest Formula 1 drivers of the 1960s. His talents weren't just limited to Formula 1, however, as he proved victorious in NASCAR, IndyCar, saloon cars, and at Le Mans. He established his own team, was a brilliant engineer, was the first F1 driver to pioneer the use of a full-face helmet, and invented the champagne-spraying celebration that is now the norm on motorsport podiums the world over.

Born in 1931, Gurney was the perfect age to become swept up in the emerging teen hot-rod culture in 1940s and 1950s America. After serving as a mechanic during the Korean War, he was well-versed in building his own cars. He competed in speed trials, drag races, and eventually sportscars, and so impressive were his early races that he was handed the opportunity to race at Le Mans in 1958. His brilliance at that most grueling of competitions caught the eye of Enzo Ferrari, who signed him to race for Ferrari in Formula 1 and complete the second half of the 1959 season. In his first three races for the Scuderia, he took two podiums, but he quickly realized that the politics of the team didn't suit him.

In 1960, he moved to BRM, but the season was a disaster, compounded by a horrible accident at the Dutch Grand Prix, where brake failure sent him into the crowd, breaking his arm and killing a spectator. For 1961, he moved to the all-new Porsche team, and in 1962, he took his, and Porsche's, first Grand Prix victory. It remains the German marque's only win in Formula 1. For 1964 and 1965, Gurney raced for Sir Jack Brabham, taking the Australian team's first Formula 1 win. Ten podiums in those two years were evidence of just how consistently brilliant the young American truly was. But Gurney wanted more.

In 1965, Gurney finally made good on a pact he and the designer, racer, and American legend Carroll Shelby had made to create their own team, All American Racers. They entered Formula 1 in 1966, partnering with British engine maker Weslake, to become known as Anglo American Racers, with their beautiful car, the Eagle Mk1. Their first victory came at the Belgian Grand Prix in 1967, where Gurney proved victorious over Jackie Stewart by more than a minute.

Gurney retired from Formula 1 in 1970 to focus on his All American Racers team, which continued to compete in America. In total, All American Racers won seventy-eight races, including the Indy 500, 24 Hours of Daytona, and 12 Hours of Sebring. Dan Gurney lived to the age of eighty-six, leaving the world with a smile on his face in 2018. Although he was not recorded as an F1 champion, his talent alone means he more than deserves his place alongside those who wore the crown. After all, of all the drivers and all the rivals whom the great Jim Clark faced, Gurney was the only one he ever truly feared.

THE 1960S

BRUCE McLAREN

In 1959, New Zealander Bruce McLaren became the youngest driver to win a Formula 1 Grand Prix, a record that would stand for four decades. He raced for Cooper for seven seasons, finishing third in the 1962 world championship before setting up his own team in 1966. He took the first victory for the McLaren team, which still bears his name, at the 1968 Belgian Grand Prix. He was a pioneer, designing and engineering revolutionary cars whose impact was felt across the world of racing and establishing a brand that defined the future of the sport. In 1970, at just thirty-two, he was killed testing one of his own cars at Goodwood.

PEDRO RODRÍGUEZ

Considered the greatest wet-weather driver of his era, Pedro Rodríguez had a combination of precision, commitment, and delicate feel that made him devastatingly quick in the most difficult of conditions. He made his name in sportscars, winning at Le Mans, Daytona, and all around the world, and he was beloved by fans of Porsche, Ferrari, and Ford alike. But his greatest win came in Formula 1, at the wheel of a BRM in wet conditions in 1970 at Spa. He lost his life racing in 1971, nine years after his younger brother Ricardo also perished at the wheel. Today, Mexico City's Grand Prix track, Autódromo Hermanos Rodríguez, is named for the country's most-loved racing sons.

JO SIFFERT

The son of a humble Swiss dairy farmer, Jo Siffert made every chance count. Few drivers of his era gave as much of themselves to their craft. Always at the limit, always on the edge, Siffert was an exhilarating entertainer behind the wheel. He was quick, too—a multiple winner of non-championship F1 races, a two-time Grand Prix winner, victorious at the Targa Florio and Daytona 24, and a two-time winner at Le Mans. After Pedro Rodríguez's death, it was Siffert who carried the BRM team in Formula 1, until he, too, was claimed by the sport he loved, at Brands Hatch in 1971 at age thirty-five.

CHRIS AMON

Despite never winning a Formula 1 Grand Prix, Chris Amon is widely and rightly held to be one of the very finest drivers of his era. The irony, of course, is that he won everywhere else: Le Mans, the World Sportscar Championship, Tasman Series, touring cars, Can-Am. He took numerous Formula 1 pole positions and podiums, and won eight non-championship F1 races. It was only when things counted for the title in Formula 1 that his talent far outweighed his luck, and 1968 should have been his year. He was mighty. Only terrible mechanical reliability stopped him and Ferrari from challenging for the crown. A gentleman and one of the very best racers of his generation, Chris Amon moved home to New Zealand in retirement and lived to the age of seventy-three.

TITANS OF THE 1960s

LOTUS

Team Lotus was the brainchild of the designer and engineer Colin Chapman, and the team defined the 1960s and 1970s in Formula 1. The outfit's innovative designs often put it at the forefront, but as Chapman pushed to make his cars ever lighter in search of greater speed, their structural fragility led to many accidents and, for many drivers, a lack of faith in their cars. The team's first win actually came from a customer, as Sir Stirling Moss won the 1960 Monaco Grand Prix in a Lotus 18 entered by Rob Walker. In 1961, Team Lotus had its first victory, courtesy of Innes Ireland. By 1963, the brilliant Lotus 25, the first F1 car to use a stressed monocoque, took Jim Clark to his first title, a feat he almost repeated in 1964, only to miss out in the final race. The new Lotus 33 brought Clark his second title in 1965, the same year he and Lotus also won the Indy 500. By 1968, the Lotus 49 was again the car to have, but Clark's death hit the team hard. Graham Hill stepped into the team-leader position and duly delivered another crown. With three driver titles and three constructor titles, Lotus was the team to beat in F1's second decade.

FERRARI

Ferrari began the 1960s on the back foot, but as soon as the new engine formula was introduced in 1961, it took the opportunity to follow the trend and build a rear-engined car—the Sharknose 156. And with a 120-degree V6 in the back, what a car it was. The 1961 title became a fight between Ferrari's drivers Wolfgang von Trips and Phil Hill. Von Trips perished at Monza; Hill won and took the crown. The 156 continued to race without its notorious sharknose into the 1960s, delivering another title to the Scuderia in 1964 with John Surtees at the wheel. But for the latter half of the decade, Ferrari won just three more Grands Prix as the unstoppable rise of the English "garagistes," whom Enzo Ferrari derided and disliked, forced Ferrari to rethink its strategy. After Surtees' success in 1964, it was more than a decade until Ferrari again won the world championship.

BRM

BRM (British Racing Motors) was established in 1945 and officially entered Formula 1 with cars and engines of its own design under the banner of the Owen Racing Organisation, named for its major benefactors. The team achieved limited success until 1960, when it promoted the former Rolls-Royce engineer Tony Rudd to take full technical control of the outfit. By 1962, the P57 was both reliable and fast; it took BRM and their driver Graham Hill to the world championship. BRM came second in the Constructors' World Championship three times in the 1960s and once in the 1970s, and their engines went on to be used by numerous teams long into the new decade.

BRABHAM

In 1960, Formula 1 World Champion Sir Jack Brabham started his own team, and in 1966, he became the first racing driver to win both driver and constructor crowns in his own car. In the 1960s, together with the designer Ron Tauranac, Brabham became the world's number-one vendor of open wheel racing cars to private entrants, building more than five hundred race cars for use in Formula 1, Formula 2, Formula 3, Formula 5000, and the Indy 500. Brabham's run of success in F1 came with the switch to 3.0-liter engines in 1966 and with their decision to partner with the Australian engineering firm Repco to repurpose old American Oldsmobile road-going V8 engines for F1 use. This brought the team back-to-back double titles in 1966 and 1967 in the nimble BT19 and BT20.

MATRA

Matra was a French racing team that had been successful in Formula 3 and Formula 2. Then in 1967, Matra's F2 car was permitted to enter the German Grand Prix, and it shocked the establishment with the third-fastest qualifying time. The team entered its own F1 car in 1968, using revolutionary structural fuel tanks inspired by their use in aviation. While the technology was banned for 1970, it ran for one final season in 1969. That year, the British team owner Ken Tyrrell took the reins, and Matra and its driver Sir Jackie Stewart were crowned world champions in the magnificent MS80, which won five of the season's eleven races.

HONDA

The Japanese company's tricky relationship with Formula 1 began in 1964, just four years after Honda had created its first road car. It shocked the sport by winning its first Grand Prix in only its second season of competition. In 1966, with the new 3.0-liter regulations, Honda designed a powerful V12 engine, which was finally allowed to shine in 1967 with a chassis designed by the British company Lola. The "Hondola" RA300 won the Italian Grand Prix that year and finished fourth in the Constructors' Championship despite having only one driver, John Surtees. After reliability problems in 1968 and the death of their driver Jo Schlesser, Honda withdrew from the sport to focus on cornering the American road car market.

RACE OF THE DECADE

1967 ITALIAN GRAND PRIX

This was a race for the ages: a close field of drivers (many of whom had or would go on to win championships), a constantly changing order, a truly epic race-long fight for the win, and one of the greatest drives of Jim Clark's all-too-short life. Clark had taken pole in his Lotus 49, but the top five spots on the grid were composed of five different teams. Sir Jack Brabham was second in the Brabham BT24, Bruce McLaren third in his McLaren BRM M5A, Chris Amon fourth in the sole Ferrari 312, and Dan Gurney fifth in his beautiful Eagle Mk1. Graham Hill lined up eighth in his Lotus, one spot ahead of John Surtees in the Honda RA300.

There was confusion from the get-go, as some drivers didn't even realize the race was being started, but through the chaos Gurney led the opening lap from Brabham, Hill, and Clark, who fought his way into the lead after only a few laps with team-mate Hill close behind in his wheel tracks. But all was not well with Clark's Lotus, and its handling quickly proved troublesome. As he pulled himself up in his cockpit to look behind, he noticed a flat rear tire. Clark pitted on lap thirteen and emerged with fresh tires, but he was now a lap behind.

What transpired from this point on was one of Jim Clark's most electrifying drives as he set about regaining the lap he'd lost. Lap after lap he danced his Lotus around the Theatre of Speed, passing the leaders to sit ahead of them on track, but still almost a full lap behind. Clark's superior pace allowed new race leader Hill to sit in his slipstream and take the tow to pull out his own lead over his rivals. Clark motored back around to the rear of the field to start making his way back through an order that seemed to change every lap. The closeness of the competition saw some truly exhilarating action from front to back. Clark, however, was on another planet as he deftly cut his way through all the way up to fourth place.

Fourth became third as Hill's engine expired from the lead, third became second as Clark blasted past Surtees, and second became the lead on lap sixty-one as Clark powered past Brabham. Having made up over a lap and extended a comfortable lead, Clark was set to have his day of days, but on the final lap his engine started to misfire, the fuel pump failing at the very last minute.

Surtees and Brabham roared past, fighting all the way around the final lap, and it was Surtees who took the win by 0.2 seconds. This became Honda's final F1 victory as a manufacturer until 2006. While the Italian fans went wild for the win of the former Ferrari champion, their salutations were equally riotous for Clark, whose Lotus spluttered over the line in third. Despite the last-lap heartache, Jim Clark had driven quite possibly his greatest ever Grand Prix.

WITH TECHNICAL REGULATIONS from an engine perspective relatively stable in the 1970s, the era became one of tremendous innovation in aerodynamics, led by the inventive minds at work in Formula 1 teams. The seemingly simple cigar-shaped cars that were the benchmark of the previous decade gave way to increasingly complex cars that utilized airflow to build grip and speed. That grip was ramped up from the very start of the decade by the introduction of slick tires. The huge contact patches created by the sleek, smooth rubber put all the power of the F1 engines onto the road. Grooved tires would only ever again be used for wet races (save for a short period in the 2000s).

Lotus again led the way in the technical revolution. The all-new Lotus 72 proved to be the first F1 design that used almost the entire car itself as a wing. Developments continued throughout the decade as variable flexible suspension, inboard brakes, and side-mounted radiators made their way into the sport. Transverse gearboxes were introduced to improve weight distribution, and enormous airboxes appeared above the drivers' helmets to direct air to the engines to help with cooling. But the wildest developments occurred in the second half of the decade. Ken Tyrrell was, by now, running his own team, whose P34 shocked the world with a radical development: it raced with six wheels, two at the back and four at the front.

While never considered superior over the entire field, its day of days was the 1976 Swedish Grand Prix, which it won.

Lotus by now was experimenting with plastic skirts around the floor edges of its cars, in preparation for a development that would change the face of the sport. In 1977, they released the Lotus 78, a striking car with sidepods that acted as wings, airflow tunnels under the car, and sliding skirts to create low pressure known as "ground effect." The dual forces of the airflow pushing the car down and the low pressure pulling the car down made its grip astronomical. The philosophy was taken to extremes in 1978 by both Lotus and Brabham, whose designer Gordon Murray created the "fan car." This F1 concept had a giant fan at the rear of the BT46B, which literally sucked the car onto the track. It won its first race, and the team immediately withdrew it rather than have it banned.

Foreshadowing the next decade of F1 tech, Renault entered the sport at the end of the 1970s and developed a 1.5-liter turbocharged engine. For more than a decade, the regulations had allowed for the smaller supercharged engines to compete alongside the 3.0-liter normally aspirated units that had become the norm, but nobody had considered their use to be of any competitive advantage. After many failures, Renault eventually made the technology work, and as the 1970s drew to a close, Formula 1 found itself on the cusp of a technological and political war between the factory teams, who could afford to devote time and money to the development of turbo technology, and the smaller independent teams, who believed aerodynamics and ground effect were the best path forward.

The political fight had its foundations in the emergingly active voice of the Formula One Constructors' Association (FOCA). Led by Brabham's new team owner Bernie Ecclestone, it represented the interests of the non-factory F1 teams, such as Lotus, Tyrrell, and McLaren, against the perceived favoritism of the sport's governing body, the FIA, toward the factory outfits of Ferrari, Renault, and Alfa Romeo. As FOCA pushed for better financial terms for their members, greater safety, and better track conditions—including medical facilities for their drivers and a more streamlined organization of races and the world championship—the battle lines were drawn for a war that would erupt at the end of the decade for both commercial and regulatory ownership of the sport.

Formula 1, for all intents and purposes, was still a largely disorganized sport. Incredibly, there was no contractual obligation for any of the teams to show up to races, and many opted not to attend various Grands Prix due to the cost or logistics. While the world championship was in its third decade, there was still no cohesive nature to its promotion, and teams still negotiated individually with circuits for their appearance money. Ecclestone convinced his fellow team bosses that they would be a more powerful voice if they acted together, especially where money was concerned.

Safety remained a key consideration. In 1970, Jochen Rindt was crowned the sport's only posthumous world champion, and while the total number of fatalities in the sport was dropping, it was still in double digits for the decade. Formula 1 was fortunate not to have lost Niki Lauda in his fiery accident at the 1976 German Grand Prix, and his incredible comeback story resulted in a championship showdown at Fuji. In addition to the drama, that Japanese race is notable for being the first Grand Prix ever to be televised live globally.

Ecclestone, more than anyone else in the sport, had a vision of what Formula 1 could become and where it could go. Emboldened by the success of the 1976 Japanese Grand Prix telecast, and having taken personal financial risks to ensure some races happened at all, he plotted a course to revolutionize the organization of the sport.

As the 1970s ended, Formula 1 found itself at a crossroads. Everything was about to change.

JOCHEN RINDT

« 1X CHAMPION »

A once-in-a-generation talent, Jochen Rindt was a truly breathtaking driver—the kind who made the impossible seem possible. He was a man born of tremendous talent, yet he would have little time to show it before it was all taken away. That his star shone so briefly in Formula 1 is one of the great tragedies in the history of the sport.

Rindt was born to an Austrian mother and a German father in Mainz, Germany, in 1942. His parents were killed in a British bombing raid during the Second World War when he was just fifteen months old. Afterward, he was raised by his grandparents in Graz, Austria, and had a troubled upbringing. He was in almost constant trouble, both at school and with the police. The joker of the crowd, he did almost anything to impress his friends and seemingly had no awareness of danger—his japes resulted in various broken bones, including his neck.

After attending the 1961 German Grand Prix, Rindt determined that motor racing was for him, and his recklessness, or courage, saw him make immediate waves. Driving his grandmother's car and racing under an Austrian license, he was disqualified from his first race. Two years later, in 1963, he started racing in Formula Junior, where he stood out for his bravery and risk-taking. It was in Formula 2, however, where he really made his name and where he would continue to race even during his Formula 1 career.

He made his Grand Prix debut for the private Rob Walker team at the Austrian Grand Prix in 1964, and he picked up a full-time seat with Cooper in 1965. Despite showing huge promise, he achieved just three podiums in his first three full-time seasons. He moved to BRM in 1968 and only finished two races, though both were on the podium. But it was to be in 1969, with Lotus, that all started to come together. Rindt took points, podiums, and eventually his first win at the US Grand Prix.

For the 1970 season, Lotus boss Colin Chapman promised Rindt the best car in the sport, and he delivered on his word. Of the opening six races of the season, Rindt won four and retired from two. He started to be concerned that things were coming too easily, that the title couldn't possibly be his for the taking. Yet it was. However, Jochen Rindt never raised the trophy and would never know what he had achieved or the regard in which he was held. During qualifying for the Italian Grand Prix, something broke on his Lotus. As the front end crumpled beneath the car, Rindt was pulled forward and killed by the belts designed to protect him.

Jochen Rindt was one of the most electrifying racers the sport had ever seen. And in 1970, having amassed so many points before his death that no driver could beat him, he was and remains its only posthumous F1 champion.

THE 1970S

105

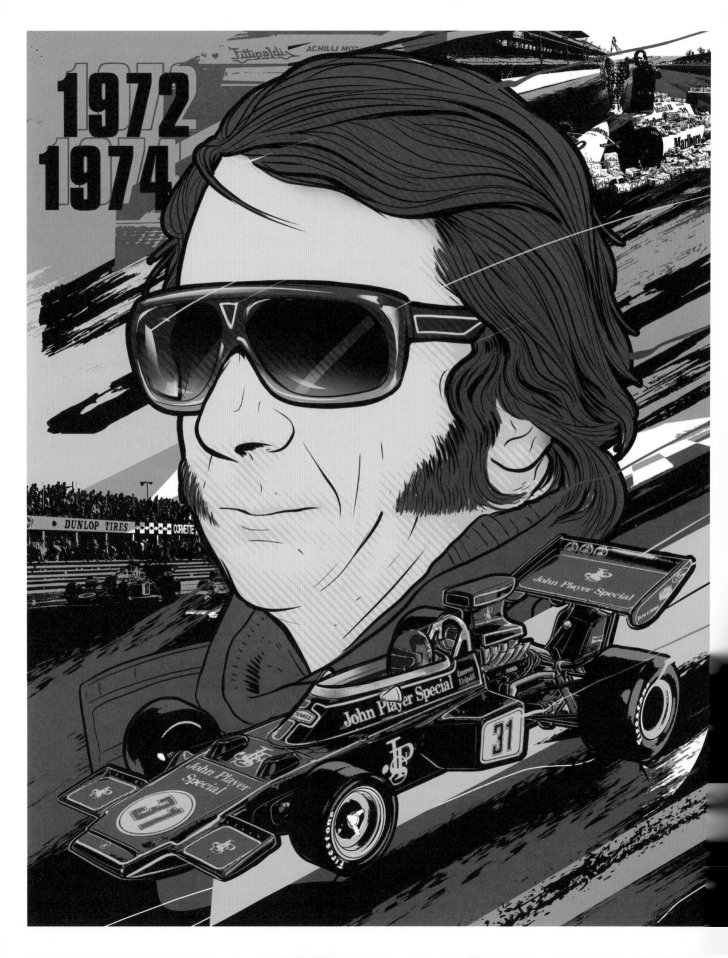

EMERSON FITTIPALDI

<< 2X CHAMPION >>

For thirty-three years, Emerson Fittipaldi held the record as the youngest world champion in Formula 1 history. His ascent to the top was meteoric, and his career in F1 bookmarked an almost perfect decade. Then after a partial retirement, he enjoyed a second career in America, where he became as beloved by fans of IndyCar as he was by those of Formula 1. To this day, his name is synonymous with a meticulous and mindful approach to racing, allied to a pure and infectious joy for the sport that framed everything he did.

As the youngest son of a Brazilian motorsport journalist and commentator, Fittipaldi was perhaps always destined for a life of high-octane thrills; it seemed only natural that he and his elder brother Wilson should compete. Their start came on two wheels and then shifted to racing speedboats, but after Wilson suffered an accident, both switched their focus to four wheels and circuit racing.

In 1968, at the age of twenty-one, Fittipaldi won the Brazilian Formula Vee title, an entry-level series of small, affordable, Volkswagen-powered single-seaters. In 1969, buoyed by his success at home, he determined to move to Europe and convince the wider world of racing that his talent merited a spot at the head table. He did so, comfortably, becoming the 1969 Formula 3 champion.

In 1970, he moved up to Formula 2, driving a Lotus, and as might be expected, his talent immediately took the attention of Colin Chapman, who asked Fittipaldi to contest some F1 races in Lotus'

third car. The young Brazilian was taken under the wing of team leader Jochen Rindt, whom Fittipaldi idolized. When the Austrian was killed and his Lotus team-mate John Miles was so profoundly affected by his passing that he quit the sport, Lotus had no option but to make their young Brazilian charge the team leader.

In the team's first race after Rindt's passing, Fittipaldi took Lotus to the top step of the podium. In 1972, they won the world championship together with an utterly spellbinding performance by the Brazilian at the wheel of the magnificent Lotus 72. After finishing second in 1973, a lucrative deal from McLaren lured him away for 1974, when he took the title for a second time. In 1975, he took second place in the championship. He was still in demand, still highly regarded, and the world remained at his feet.

But in 1976, his career stalled as he embarked on the folly of team ownership with his brother. He never won a Grand Prix again. He only saw the podium twice more. He retired without the fanfare his arrival and success deserved. But three years later, he was back behind the wheel for a second thirteen-year career in America, where he won the Indy 500 twice and the IndyCar championship itself in 1989.

One of the great champions and ambassadors of the sport, he still tours the world as an avid and passionate fan of all motorsport events, especially those races contested by his children, nephews, and grandchildren.

THE 1970S

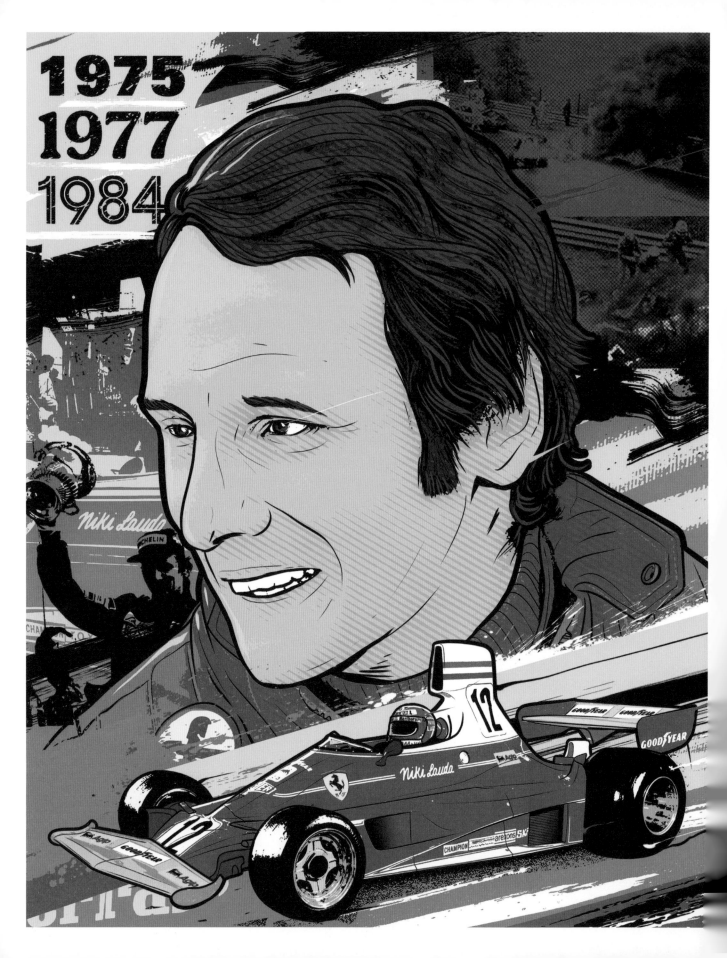

NIKI LAUDA

« 3X CHAMPION »

When Hollywood came looking for a real-life Formula 1 career fit for the silver screen, they found it in the story of Niki Lauda. The sharp-tongued and sharp-minded Austrian was a man you crossed at your peril. Ruthlessly determined and unfathomably resilient, his destiny led him to motorsport, a calling that almost killed him but that ultimately secured his place as one of the all-time greats.

Lauda was born into a wealthy family in Austria in 1949. But his love of racing was an embarrassment to his parents, and he was forced to embark on his career without their financial backing. Instead, Lauda used his persuasive acumen to attain bank loans that took him from season to season.

He began his career in Formula 1 as what we would today call a "pay driver," financing teams to allow him to race their cars. Although initially he found himself on the wrong teams at the wrong time, his pace became undeniable. His no-nonsense approach infuriated as many as it impressed. When he was called up to test for Ferrari, he told the great Enzo Ferrari that his car was "shit." The old man loved Lauda's attitude, and in 1974, they won two Grands Prix together. In 1975, Lauda and Ferrari proved unstoppable in the fantastic 312T, winning five races and taking the podium in three more, which led them to a world championship, Ferrari's first since John Surtees' eleven years earlier.

In 1976, Lauda started on a similar footing: five wins in nine races, three podiums, and one retirement. Only McLaren's James Hunt looked even vaguely likely of challenging what would surely be the Austrian's second title. But then came Germany and Lauda's horrific crash on the second lap. The brutality of the impact tore his helmet from his face, and his car was engulfed in flames. When he was pulled from the wreckage by his fellow drivers, his injuries were so bad that he was given the last rites by a priest.

However, Lauda survived and returned to the cockpit just six weeks later, finishing fourth at Monza, his scars bleeding through the bandages under his helmet. Despite Ferrari's doubts about his ability to perform after his accident, Lauda won the world championship for a second time in 1977, quitting the team immediately afterwards in an ultimate rebuke of their misgivings. He joined Brabham, winning a couple of races, but then he retired before the end of the 1979 season. Yet Lauda's competitive desires remained undimmed, and he returned to Formula 1 in 1982 with McLaren, winning his third world championship in 1984 before quitting for good at the end of 1985.

Lauda went on to become a much-respected voice within the sport, employed as a key advisor to Ferrari and Jaguar. However, his impact was felt most deeply at Mercedes—where his leadership formed the foundation for that team's decade of domination in the sport.

Niki Lauda died at the age of seventy in 2019, mourned by a nation and a sport he invigorated at every turn.

THE 1970S

109

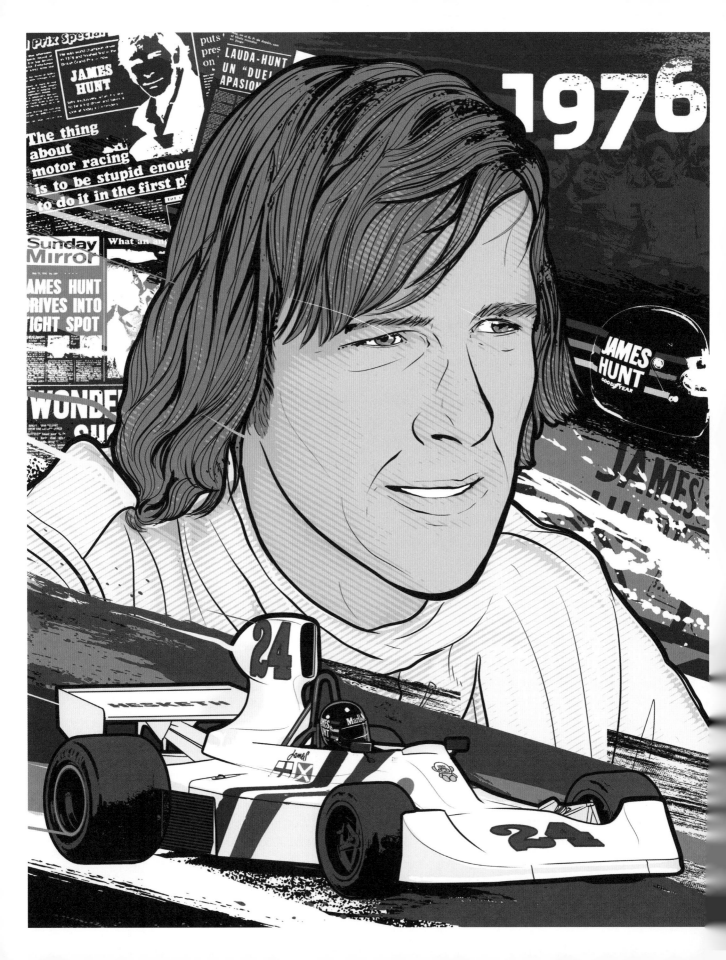

JAMES HUNT

<< 1X CHAMPION >>

If Hollywood found its hero in Niki Lauda, its antihero was James Hunt. Loud, unapologetic, and boisterous, he partied hard and raced even harder. He was the darling of the tabloids and the scourge of the motorsport press, but the truth was that racing terrified him. Yet on his day, he could rise to beat the very best of his generation.

Born in Surrey, England, in 1947, Hunt was privately educated and by all accounts a handful. His rebellious nature made him impossible to tame, and with an impressive build, long blond hair, and film-star good looks, he gave the impression of the ultimate bad boy who proved irresistible to women. He initially showed promise in racket sports, but a chance invitation to watch a friend race at Silverstone saw Hunt catch the motorsport bug.

He was a nervous competitor who was known to vomit before races, yet once in the heat of the action, he proved brave, quick, and, all too often, wild. So much so he soon earned the nickname "Hunt the shunt" due to his numerous crashes. Controversy and James Hunt were rarely far apart, yet with multiple wins and lap records he climbed the English national ladder to Formula 3. F1, however, appeared a step too far.

In fact, the chances of him ever making it to Formula 1 might not have arisen were it not for the emergence of the Hesketh Racing team. Founded by Lord Alexander Hesketh, a young English aristocrat who had inherited a fortune and seemed intent on spending it all, Hesketh Racing was all about having fun. It was joked that the team spent as much on champagne as it did on petrol, and the sheer number of beautiful women it invited to races often outnumbered race team staff.

Hunt ran some Formula 2 races with the team in 1972, but by 1973 Lord Hesketh had decided to enter Formula 1, and Hunt went with him. While members of the establishment looked down their noses at Hesketh, the team created an aura of eccentric fun that has resonated through the history of motorsport. Despite not having the budget or know-how of the top teams, Hunt and Hesketh roared to victory in the 1975 Dutch Grand Prix in a straight fight with Niki Lauda and Ferrari. By the end of the season, Hesketh was out of money, but Hunt had an offer on the table from McLaren.

The stars aligned, and in 1976, a maturing Hunt and McLaren were the only ones to consistently compete with Lauda. Their battle became the stuff of legend, particularly after Lauda's near-fatal crash at the German Grand Prix. The championship fight came down to the last race in Japan, but in terrible conditions, Lauda determined it was too dangerous to carry on. Hunt persevered, taking the points he needed to be crowned world champion.

After a couple more seasons, Hunt retired in 1979 to become an outspoken and popular television commentator. With his world calming down after two failed marriages, he settled into life as a father, which he adored.

But, in 1993, with his life in the happiest place he could remember, he suffered a sudden heart attack and died at just forty-five years of age.

THE 1970S

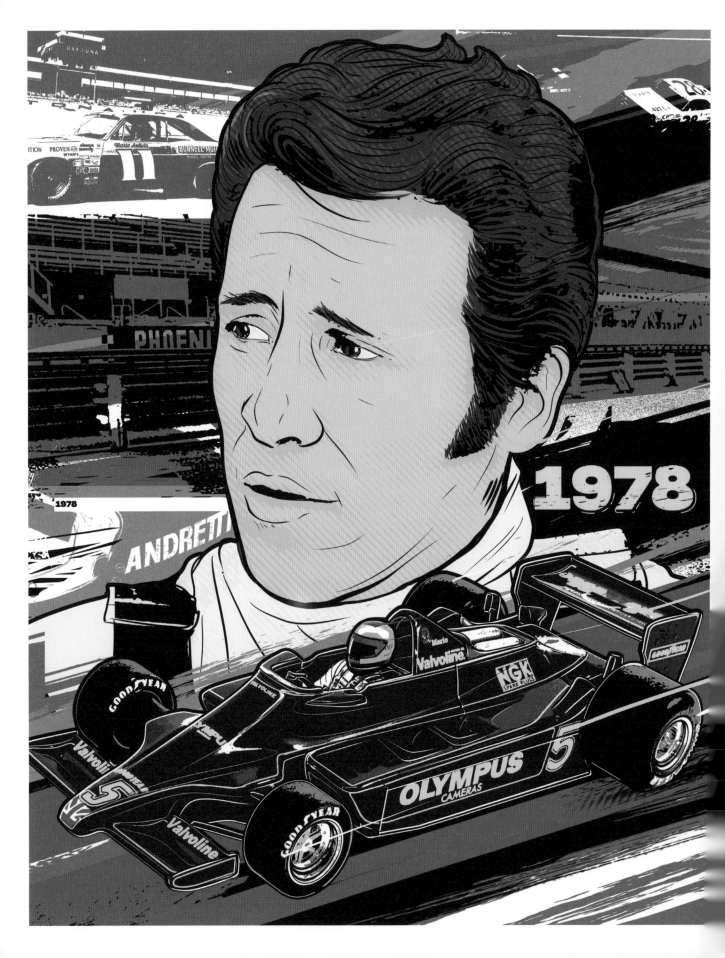

MARIO ANDRETTI

《《 1X CHAMPION 》》

Some sportspeople become so revered within their game, so entwined with the core of what their sport represents and what it is to be deemed truly great, that their name becomes synonymous with it. Think Michael Jordan for basketball, Pele for soccer, Tom Brady for American football.... For motorsport, that man is Mario Andretti.

He and his twin brother Aldo were born in Italy in 1940 in the midst of the Second World War. The Andretti family spent over a decade in refugee camps, as their home became part of the new Yugoslavia. Aldo and Mario fell in love with racing while still young children, catching a glimpse of the Mille Miglia and getting a chance visit to the 1954 Italian Grand Prix at Monza, where Mario witnessed firsthand the genius of his hero Alberto Ascari.

The family emigrated to America in 1955, and after forging their licenses to appear older than they were, the Andretti brothers started racing a Hudson Hornet on American dirt tracks. Both proved fast, but a terrible accident stopped Aldo's racing career on the spot. Mario, however, couldn't be contained and proved to be adaptable, dogged, and ever so fast. He won in midgets, sprint cars, NASCAR, the Daytona 500, drag racing, the Pikes Peak hillclimb—you name it. If Mario raced it, he could win it.

The call of open wheel racing pulled Mario to IndyCar. He won the Indy 500 in 1969 and the IndyCar championship in 1965, 1966, and 1969. But Mario had always dreamed of Formula 1, and after impressing Colin Chapman at the 1965 Indy

500, he was offered a race seat at the Lotus team anytime he wanted. He made his debut for Lotus at the 1968 US Grand Prix and duly put the car on pole. He had to retire with a clutch issue, though, and thereafter made only sporadic appearances over the next few years for March, Parnelli, and Ferrari, winning his first Grand Prix in South Africa in 1971 for the Scuderia. Then, in 1976, Chapman finally convinced Andretti to commit full-time to Formula 1 and leave IndyCar behind.

Andretti took the leap of faith and worked closely with Chapman to hone the design of the Lotus into a world-beater. They came third in 1977, and in 1978—at the wheel of the Lotus 79—there was no stopping Andretti; he became champion of the world. As Lotus slipped off the pace into the 1980s, Andretti moved to Alfa Romeo and then Ferrari. After one final pole position and podium for the Scuderia at Monza in 1982, Andretti returned to America, where he continued racing in IndyCar until his mid-fifties. He won the American title once more in 1984.

Of all racers, Mario came the closest to emulating Graham Hill's Triple Crown: In 1995, at the age of fifty-five, he finished first in class but second overall at the 24 Hours of Le Mans. Today, even in his eighties, Andretti is still happiest behind the wheel, taking lucky guests and competition winners for two-seater rides around the IndyCar tracks of the world at more than 200 mph. He is rightly revered as one of the greatest racers who ever lived.

THE 1970S

JODY SCHECKTER

<< 1X CHAMPION >>

Few in racing circles believed Jody Scheckter would ever become a Formula 1 World Champion. At the start of his career, he was too reckless; at the end of his career, he was too soft. And yet, against all the odds, one last roll of the dice with the biggest team in the sport saw it all come together for him. His F1 career lasted less than a decade, but in that time he cemented his place in history as an unforgiving and unforgettable champion.

Born in 1950 in East London, South Africa, the young Scheckter worked as an apprentice and learned to drive at the Renault dealership his father owned. Racing was a natural development for him, but in his first saloon car race, he was disqualified for dangerous driving. Scheckter only knew how to drive one way, and his style was as wild and reckless as it was impressively quick. And so it proved through Formula Ford and Formula 3, as his on-track reputation became allied to a forthright and unapologetic personality that could rub people the wrong way.

Despite their trepidation over Scheckter's reputational tendency to overdo things, McLaren signed him for occasional Formula 1 races through 1972 and 1973. He was involved in some serious incidents, one taking out reigning champion Emerson Fittipaldi, and one at the start of the 1973 British Grand Prix in which he was responsible for an accident that wiped out almost the entire field in what remains one of Formula 1's biggest crashes ever. The drivers agreed Scheckter was a danger

and should be banned, but McLaren instead opted to rest him for a few races.

During the 1973 season, he signed to race for Tyrrell in 1974, but the death of François Cevert, who would have been his team-mate, at the 1973 season-ending US Grand Prix, had a massive effect on him. Scheckter was the first on the scene, and the violence of Cevert's death forever changed the way he raced. Never again did he take the risks he once had. Helped by mentor Ken Tyrrell, Scheckter calmed his aggression but maintained his car control and electrifying pace to win his first two Grands Prix. In 1974 and 1976, he finished third in the championship. In 1977, he moved to Walter Wolf Racing and duly finished second in the championship, running Lauda and Ferrari close for the title. So close that Ferrari offered Scheckter a seat for 1979.

While many assumed that the South African's short temper and direct, often confrontational communication style was ill-suited to life at Ferrari, the duo were a perfect match. Scheckter was crowned the 1979 Formula 1 World Champion, and along with team-mate Gilles Villeneuve, Ferrari went one-two in the championship. It would be Ferrari's last world title for twenty years.

When his contract ended at the conclusion of the 1980 season, Scheckter retired. Today, he lives in England and runs an award-winning biodynamic farm, famous for its meat and buffalo dairy products.

THE 1970S

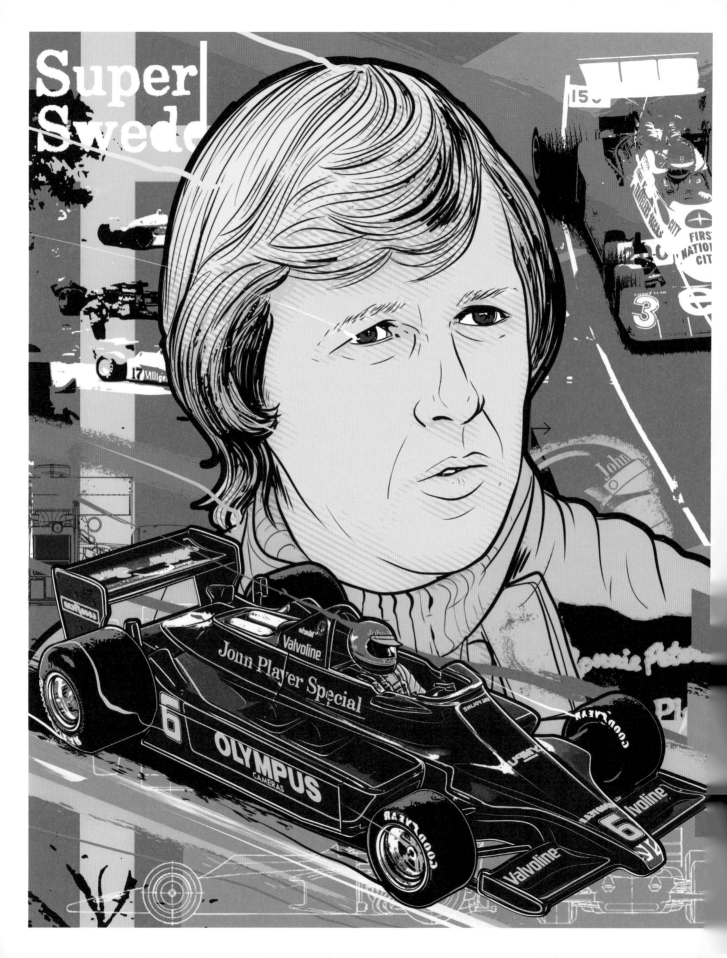

RONNIE PETERSON

Ronnie Peterson was one of the fastest racers of the 1970s. His skill was so pure and his manner so charming that there wasn't a person in motorsport who didn't love him. Mesmerizing on track and delightful away from it, he had everything it took to be a world champion, except time. His death at the 1978 Italian Grand Prix left the racing world in shock.

Born near Orebro, Sweden, in 1944, Peterson began his career on the now traditional and accepted path of kart racing. He was impressive from the start and soon graduated to Formula 3, winning titles in 1968 and 1969 in a car he had designed with his father, a baker. But his next racing season, 1970, broke all the perceived rules of the ladder system. He moved up to race in Formula 2 but was considered to be so talented that he also raced in Formula 1.

The super-fast "SuperSwede" made such an immediate impact that he was moved to the official factory March team for 1971 to compete in both Formula 2 and Formula 1. He won the Formula 2 title and came second in the Formula 1 World Championship. It was an astonishing achievement at the time, and even more incredible when one considers his relative inexperience compared to the might of the two championship fields he competed against.

In 1973, he moved to Lotus and partnered Emerson Fittipaldi, taking his first win at the French Grand Prix. He followed it up with three more wins across the season. But Lotus started to fall off the pace. Indeed, the 1974 Lotus 76 was so unpopular with its drivers that they reverted to the 1973 car, the Lotus 72, which continued to race into 1975. With no turnaround in sight, Peterson returned to March after the first race of 1976, then moved to Tyrrell for 1977.

In 1978, Colin Chapman convinced Peterson that the tide had turned and the Lotus was again the car to have. As it turned out, he was absolutely correct. But as part of the deal, Peterson was expected to back up Mario Andretti. Peterson would be the number two, and if the cars found themselves leading the race, it was expected that Andretti would win. Peterson duly obliged, often finishing on Andretti's tail to make a point about his speed and the orders he was under. He won twice in the season, once when Andretti's car failed and once when he proved so blisteringly fast that he lapped his team leader.

Peterson believed that by playing the team game he'd be next in line to fight for the title. But his time ran out. A crash at the start of the 1978 Italian Grand Prix left him with multiple fractures and burns to his legs. His injuries weren't considered life-threatening, but overnight complications proved otherwise. Come Monday morning, the unfathomable news broke that Ronnie Peterson, one of the most gifted drivers of his generation, had died. His name remains etched into memory as a racer who could and should have been a Formula 1 World Champion.

THE 1970S

117

JACKY ICKX

Charming, handsome, and sporting his trademark Elvis sunglasses, Jacky Ickx was one of the undisputed kings of 1970s F1 cool. But he was also probably the most complete driver of the era. A multiple-race winner who danced his cars through the most awful conditions, he excelled at Le Mans, too, winning the famous race a staggering six times. The Belgian won eight Grands Prix and took twenty-five podiums in an F1 career that lasted from 1966 to 1979 and saw him race for all the top teams—from Lotus to Ferrari and from McLaren to an early Williams.

CLAY REGAZZONI

It's rare for a driver to get their Formula 1 debut with Ferrari, and rarer still to score their first win at the Italian Grand Prix at Monza. But that was how Swiss driver Clay Regazzoni's F1 career began in 1970; for the season, he finished third in the championship. He took all but one of his five F1 wins for Ferrari and came second in the title race in 1974. His final race win was the very first for the Williams team in 1979. A crash at Long Beach in 1980 left him paralyzed from the waist down, but he continued to race with hand controls, promoting equal opportunity for disabled racers. He was killed in a road accident in 2006 at the age of sixty-seven.

CARLOS REUTEMANN

Carlos Reutemann, with his dashing looks and broad smile, was one of the kings of 1970s Formula 1. The Argentine driver won races for Brabham, Ferrari, and Williams and came within a point of the world championship in his penultimate season in 1981. For three decades, he was the only Formula 1 driver to have also stood on the podium in the World Rally Championship, a perfect example of his versatility. In retirement, Reutemann moved into politics, proving deeply popular and winning various seats and positions of power in Argentina. He died in office after suffering an intestinal hemorrhage in 2021 at age seventy-nine.

LELLA LOMBARDI

Lella Lombardi is the only woman in Formula 1 history to score points, which she did at the Spanish Grand Prix in 1974. Her F1 career saw the Italian race for March, Williams, and Brabham, becoming an inspiration to countless female and LGBTQ+ racers around the world.

DIVINA GALICIA

Divina Galicia captained the British women's ski team at two Olympic games, but after a guest spot in a celebrity car race, she fell in love with motorsport. She attempted to qualify for three Grands Prix, but her real success came in Britain's Aurora AFX Formula One series, in which she took multiple podiums.

TITANS OF THE 1970s

LOTUS

Lotus continued its excellent form into the 1970s, winning four world championships. But while its innovative cars continued to set trends, its decade of dominance was bookended with tragedy. Colin Chapman and Tony Rudd's combined expertise were harnessing ground effect and turning the entire car into a wing, using skirts to reduce to almost nothing the gap between the floor and the track, pulling the car down to generate grip. The Lotus 72 was a masterpiece of innovation and took the team to thirty-nine podiums, twenty race wins, and three Constructors' titles. But at its wheel Jochen Rindt perished, becoming the sport's only posthumous world champion. Their Lotus 78 and follow-up 79 brought them and Mario Andretti the 1978 titles, but the season and the decade ended in heartache with the tragic death of Ronnie Peterson.

FERRARI

The Scuderia started the decade strongly with the 312B in 1970, but lean years from 1971 to 1973 resulted in a key change at the top, as Ferrari employed the services of the brilliant young businessman Luca di Montezemolo to lead their F1 operations. Together with Mauro Forghieri at the helm of the team's technical department, Ferrari developed the 312 B3-74, and with Niki Lauda at the wheel, they built the foundations for the outfit's huge run of success in the decade. From 1975, the Scuderia won four Constructors' World Championships, the first in 1975 with the fabulous 312T. The 312 T2 took the honors in 1976 despite Lauda's horrific accident at the Nürburgring, and Ferrari again took constructors' and drivers' glories in 1977. Lauda left to be replaced by Gilles Villeneuve, while Jody Scheckter rounded out the decade for Ferrari with his own title in 1979, Ferrari's fourth of the 1970s.

TYRRELL

Ken Tyrrell's small British team did the unthinkable in Formula 1 and ruled the sport from a humble shed in rural England. At the turn of the decade, having run the French Matra team to championship success, Tyrrell opted to run a March chassis with a Ford Cosworth DFV engine, developing their own car in the background for an assault on the 1971 season. The car made its debut at the end of 1970, and what Tyrrell learned from the first races led to the development of the car that would win both drivers' and constructors' world titles the next year. With Sir Jackie Stewart struck down by illness in 1972, the team returned to form in 1973, as Stewart won his third and final title. But the death of the team's much-loved second driver François Cevert in the final race of the season saw Tyrrell withdraw from the event and Lotus win the constructors' crown. After Stewart's retirement, the team continued with multiple race victories throughout the era, but it was never again the force it had been in the early years of the decade.

McLAREN

Bruce McLaren created his eponymous Formula 1 team in 1966 and swept to his first win for his own team at Belgium in 1968. But he would never see the incredible heights his team would achieve, as he lost his life in a testing accident in 1970. American Teddy Mayer took over the day-to-day team operations, and competing in Formula 1, IndyCar, and Can-Am, McLaren became a global force, winning the Indy 500 in 1972 and 1974. That 1974 season was a historic one for the squad. With Emerson Fittipaldi at the wheel of the brilliant M23, he was crowned Formula 1 World Champion and McLaren Constructors' Champion. The car stayed in service for some years, and despite not achieving another team title, it took James Hunt to the drivers' crown in 1976.

WILLIAMS

Sir Frank Williams was a racing enthusiast who partnered with his friend, the racer Piers Courage, to take him to Formula 1 in a privately run Brabham in 1969. Williams launched his own team in 1970, buying chassis and engines to build his own cars until a partnership with Walter Wolf saw the team name changed and Williams himself pushed out. He reacted by setting up Williams Grand Prix Engineering for the 1977 F1 season. With designer Patrick Head, the squad made steady progress, the first true car of their own design hitting the track in 1978. In 1979, Williams adopted the ground-effect philosophy sweeping the sport and took their first win at their home race at Silverstone. With increasing confidence and know-how, Williams ended the 1970s as the team on the rise.

BRABHAM

The team's decade truly began in 1972 after Brabham had been sold to the businessman Bernie Ecclestone for £100,000. Ecclestone placed Gordon Murray in charge of design, and the young engineer's creativity flowed, building brilliant race-winning cars. His genius was often born of necessity because, while Ecclestone had negotiated a free engine deal, it was for the heavy if powerful Alfa Romeo flat-12. Murray was forced to come up with ingenious solutions to the weight deficit of the car. As he experimented with ground effect and the controversial fan car, Ecclestone and Murray placed Brabham in prime position to fight for top honors again in the 1980s.

MARCH

A team that existed for less than a decade, March nevertheless made a huge impact. In 1970, after building an F3 car in 1969, the outfit designed cars for sale in F1, F2, F3, Formula Ford, and Can-Am, as well as running their own teams in open wheel's top three tiers. March's cars remained popular with customers throughout the decade, although the factory team itself recorded just two Formula 1 wins in its history. It withdrew from the sport in 1977, but it made partial returns in later decades. Under the guise of Leyton House in the 1990s, the team gave a break to the promising young designer Adrian Newey.

RACE OF THE DECADE

1971 ITALIAN GRAND PRIX

The final Grand Prix to be held on the pure Monza circuit, before chicanes punctuated the flat-out flow of the original track, the 1971 Italian Grand Prix was an incredible duel, as a group of drivers who had never won a Formula 1 race battled for glory. The finish remains the closest in Formula 1 history, and the race is long remembered as a true classic.

Chris Amon had taken pole for Matra, denying the local Tifosi their Ferrari pole, but the Scuderia's Jacky Ickx was at least on the front row. His team-mate Clay Regazzoni could only muster eighth position on the grid, but a blistering start saw the Swiss racer take the lead ahead of compatriot Jo Siffert in the BRM. Jackie Stewart was in the mix in his Tyrrell, as was his team-mate François Cevert, along with Ronnie Peterson in his March and the BRMs of Howden Ganley and Peter Gethin. After just a few laps, motorcycle ace Mike Hailwood was in the thick of the action in his Surtees.

In those days, no one thought of conserving tires or of holding back. The leading pack was driving flat out, passing, repassing, and using slipstreams to weave, dive, and glide around one another millimeters apart in a glorious demonstration of all-out racing. Stewart would lead, Peterson, too. But the crowds went wild for the scarlet Ferrari of Regazzoni dicing at the front and leading the pack. Ickx and Siffert were soon cut back by car troubles, and when Stewart's engine blew, Cevert remained the only Tyrrell in the race. When Regazzoni's motor followed Stewart's and expired, you might have expected the Ferrari fans to have departed Monza en masse. But they stayed, transfixed by what was unraveling in front of them.

By lap twenty-five, Hailwood, the two-wheeled champion, was leading the race. With his problems seemingly fixed, Siffert retook the lead before the car locked itself into fourth gear and removed him from the duel. Cevert, Hailwood, and Peterson were now joined by pole sitter Amon, but as he removed a tear-off strip from his visor, the whole protective shield was pulled from his helmet. Barely able to see, he refused to be slowed until his engine started to fail, dropping him to sixth. All the while, Peter Gethin was making his way into the pack, and on lap fifty-two he took the lead of the race for the first time. Starting the fifty-fifth and final lap, it was now a shootout between four drivers who had never won a Grand Prix—Gethin, Peterson, Hailwood, and Cevert—and any of them could win.

Cevert led on the run down to Parabolica, but out of his slipstream and under braking, it was Peterson who took the advantage into the final corner. The crowd held its breath to see who would emerge from under the trees in the lead, and to their shock it was Gethin. He crossed the line 0.01 seconds ahead of Peterson, with Cevert a further 0.08 back. Hailwood was fourth, less than 0.2 off the win, with Ganley fifth, a further 0.4 behind the Surtees. There had never been a race like it. There never would be again.

THE
198

FORMULA 1 BEGAN THE 1980S in the midst of a fight for its future, as the two most politically powerful bodies in its organization fought for control. F1's governing body, the FIA, was by now trying desperately to retain its grip on the sport, its controversial and divisive leader Jean-Marie Balestre attempting at every turn to destabilize the unity of the Formula One Constructors' Association (FOCA).

Rising political pressure saw threats of boycotts by teams and drivers as Balestre created new rules to aid the teams loyal to the FIA and hurt those aligned with FOCA. When only the FOCA teams turned up to the 1980 Spanish Grand Prix, it was immediately deemed to be an illegal race by the FIA. As negotiations continued, Balestre announced that, from 1981, the world championship would take the form of a new FIA-sanctioned series. This meant that race organizers now had to sign on to the FIA's terms to be included in the championship, and all teams had to agree to contest the full season under the FIA's regulation.

The period was framed on one side by Balestre and on the other by FOCA's leader Bernie Ecclestone and his legal advisor Max Mosley, a former racer and one of the founding partners of the March F1 team. When the new proposals were put to FOCA in mid-1980, the organization announced their intention to withdraw from Formula 1 and establish their own world championship, the World Federation of Motor Sport. But as sponsors and suppliers started to pull away from teams on both sides, both the FIA and FOCA realized that making a deal was the only way to save not only the sport but themselves.

Their negotiations led to the drafting of an organizational and regulatory framework known as the Concorde Agreement. This was first signed in 1981 and has governed Formula 1 under various revisions ever since. Crucially, in this first agreement, only FOCA-approved tracks could apply for world championship status, giving Ecclestone huge power within the new order. The agreement gave the teams the right to help shape the technical regulations, as minimum timescales for rule changes were enacted and unanimous agreement by the teams made compulsory for their application. The rules also declared for the first time that teams must be constructors in their own right, and thus the Concorde Agreement killed off the privateers who had, until then, been able to run cars they'd bought. Despite continuing fallouts in its early years, the agreement stuck and relative peace was declared.

Ground effect was banned for safety reasons, and as a result, Formula 1 entered the turbo era. Over the next decade, Formula 1 saw the most powerful cars in its history, with the BMW engine reportedly hitting 1300 bhp in qualifying for the 1986 Italian Grand Prix. Alongside advances in engine technology, electronics formed a parallel route of development as Lotus pioneered a revolution in active suspension, by which the car automatically raised and lowered itself corner by corner to optimize its aerodynamics. Semiautomatic gearboxes were designed, and traction control was developed. Four-wheel drive and in-race refueling were both banned.

Car construction changed, too. After the unraced Lotus 88 had displayed the lightweight strength of carbon fiber, McLaren and its designer John Barnard released the MP4/1, the first F1 racing car to use a monocoque chassis made entirely from carbon fiber. With new regulations creating a survival cell around the driver, the use of carbon fiber quickly became the norm—thin but incredibly strong, it increased driver safety while also producing lighter and thus faster cars.

McLaren, along with Williams and Brabham, became the teams to beat in the 1980s, dividing all but two driver and team championships between them; Ferrari grabbed the constructor crowns in 1982 and 1983. It was an era of incredible racing and incredible champions. McLaren's two stars, Alain Prost and Ayrton Senna, wrote their own headlines as the sport's most notorious rivals. Their battles, both on and off track, held the world's attention.

The calendar was now set at around sixteen races, and while still predominantly based in Europe, the season featured popular yearly visits to Australia, Brazil, Japan, the United States,

Mexico, and Canada. Medical facilities at racetracks became compulsory in 1980, and while the sport remained dangerous, there were only four fatalities over the entire decade: two in testing in 1980 and 1986, and two at Grand Prix events, both in 1982. Formula 1 was now a globally televised, marketable sport that, thanks to constant advancements, offered enthralling races conducted, so everyone believed, in relative safety.

As the era drew to a close, the increasingly fast turbo engines were outlawed, and discussions started to take place over restricting the use of electronic "driver aids." Politically, Balestre was finding himself increasingly marginalized. Mosley had been elected as head of the FIA's Manufacturer's Commission and began to wield increasing influence within the sport's governing body.

For his part, Ecclestone had left team ownership by the end of the decade, as he was appointed the FIA's vice president of promotional affairs. He created Formula One Promotions and Administration (FOPA), which under a new Concorde Agreement written in 1987 agreed to manage television rights on behalf of the FIA and to handle all distribution of prize money to the teams.

Within a few years, Mosley was FIA president and Ecclestone controlled all the commercial elements of Formula 1. The changes in the 1980s were expected to set the stage for the 1990s to be a period of unlimited growth and positivity.

ALAN JONES

《 1X CHAMPION 》

The first world champion for the Williams Formula 1 team, Alan Jones became the unbreakable barometer by which all future Williams drivers would be measured. He was seen for much of his career as something of a midfield journeyman racer, but his tenacity and sheer force of will left a lasting impression.

Born in Melbourne, Australia, in 1946, Jones wanted to follow in the footsteps of his father, a racing driver who won the Formula Libre Australian Grand Prix in 1959. Realizing his future lay in Europe if he wanted to make a real career of racing, Jones relocated to England. With little money to his name, as his father hit bankruptcy, Jones soldiered on, racing battered old machinery in Formula Ford and Formula 3.

Success finally started to come in 1973 when he finished second in the British F3 championship, but the year was filled with heartache as Jones' beloved father passed away. With a second-place championship finish in Formula Atlantic in 1974, Jones moved up to Formula 1 in 1975. However, since he'd failed to set the world alight on his way to the top, his choices were always limited to teams on the decline; he drove for Hesketh, then for Graham Hill and John Surtees. Then in 1977, after the tragedy of Tom Pryce's death, the door opened for Jones at the Shadow team, and he repaid their faith with his debut win that same year in Austria.

His performances garnered interest from Ferrari for 1978, but when Enzo signed Gilles Villeneuve instead, Jones ended up at Williams. They were a match made in heaven, sharing a no-nonsense racing ethos grounded in dogged determination and hard work. They got a podium together at the tail end of 1978, and by mid-1979—in the all-new FW07—Jones and Williams were the class of Formula 1. They won four of the last six races of the season to enter 1980 as favorites for the crown.

In the fourteen races of the 1980 season, the car finished eleven races, and of those, five were wins and five others were podiums. Jones and Williams were champions of the world. They came in third together in the 1981 season, after which Jones retired. He missed racing, though, and went on to run a Grand Prix in 1983 and a few in 1985. He made his one and only IndyCar start in 1985, too, sensationally taking a podium on debut. But a full-season return to Formula 1 in 1986 resulted in just two points finishes, and so he returned to Australia to run a farm.

The competitive instinct remained, and Jones ran in touring cars and Aussie V8s all the way into the 2000s. While Alan Jones is not a champion who will be remembered for his grace and artistry behind the wheel, what he lacked in finesse he more than made up for in guts and a fighting instinct to win, which took him to the top of the world.

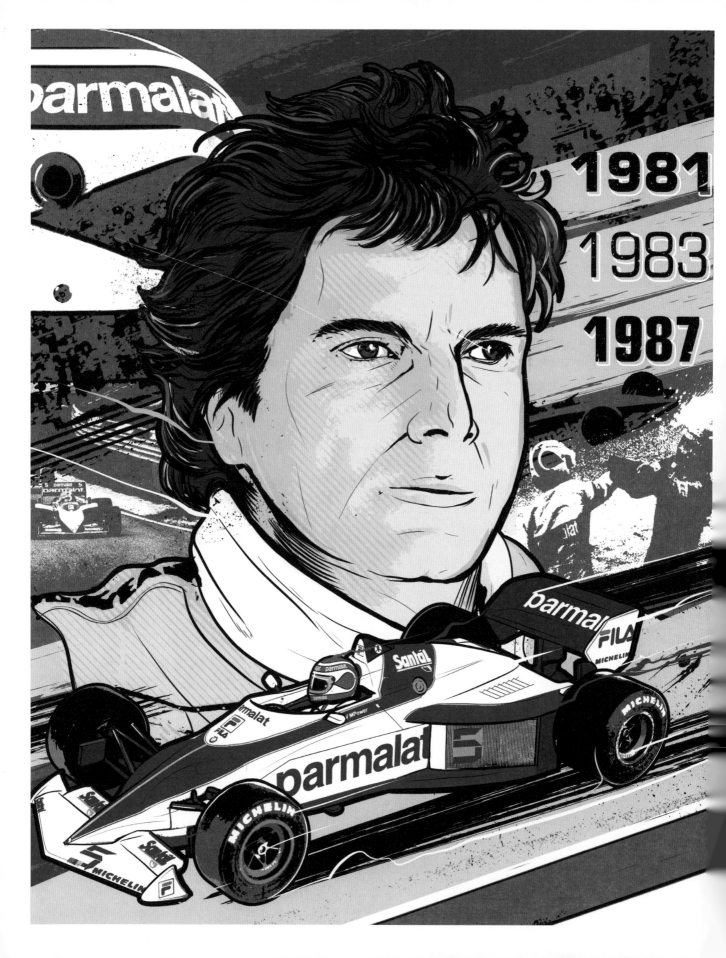

NELSON PIQUET

« 3X CHAMPION »

Nelson Piquet only ever cared about one thing, and that was winning Grands Prix. Lazy by his own admission, he nevertheless worked well enough with his engineers and mechanics and raced with enough intelligence and raw speed to take the Formula 1 World Championship three times. He was provocative throughout his career, and his racing legacy has in recent years been dented by a spate of personal controversies.

Born in Rio de Janeiro, Brazil, in 1952, Piquet could have become a professional tennis player, but after years of training, he left it all behind to pursue his dream of racing, using his mother's surname so his parents wouldn't discover what he was up to. He won karting championships and the Formula Vee title before arriving in Europe in 1977 hailed as a prodigy. He cemented the reputation in 1978 by breaking Jackie Stewart's record for most wins in a British Formula 3 season.

Brabham F1 team boss Bernie Ecclestone saw something he liked in Piquet and signed him to the team in 1979, to learn under Niki Lauda. When the great Austrian retired at the end of the season, Piquet became team leader, working with legendary designer Gordon Murray to perfect his BT49 into a championship-winning car. They won races throughout 1980, but it was in 1981 that they dominated to seal the crown. At the wheel of the BT52 in 1983, Piquet and Brabham became two-time champions.

Piquet believed he was worth more than Ecclestone was paying him and requested double his salary. When Ecclestone refused, Frank Williams offered Piquet triple, and so began a tumultuous few years between the Brazilian and his new team-mate Nigel Mansell. The duo hated each other to a distracting degree, so much so that they let the championship slip through their grasp in 1986.

Piquet managed to keep his focus in 1987 to become a three-time champion, but subsequent moves to Lotus and finally Benetton never saw him regain that title-winning spark. He quit at the end of 1991, and after sustaining major injuries in a crash attempting to qualify for the 1992 Indy 500, he quit racing altogether. He retired holding some of the most impressive statistics in F1 history: twenty-three wins, twenty-three fastest laps, twenty-four pole positions, and sixty podiums in a career that lasted just over a decade.

Although he became a successful businessman in his post-F1 years, Piquet was never far from controversy. He famously defamed team-mate Nigel Mansell's wife, claimed that Ayrton Senna was little more than a "São Paulo taxi driver," and publicly joked about Senna's death. In later years he became closely aligned with Brazil's controversial right-wing president Jair Bolsonaro, and he had his own taxi taunt turned on him by some Brazilian people as he became known as "Bolsonaro's Uber driver." His true nadir came in the 2020s, however, when he used racist and homophobic language in an interview he conducted about Sir Lewis Hamilton. The shocking comments resulted in a fine of a million dollars, and Piquet was banned from returning to a Formula 1 paddock.

THE 1980S

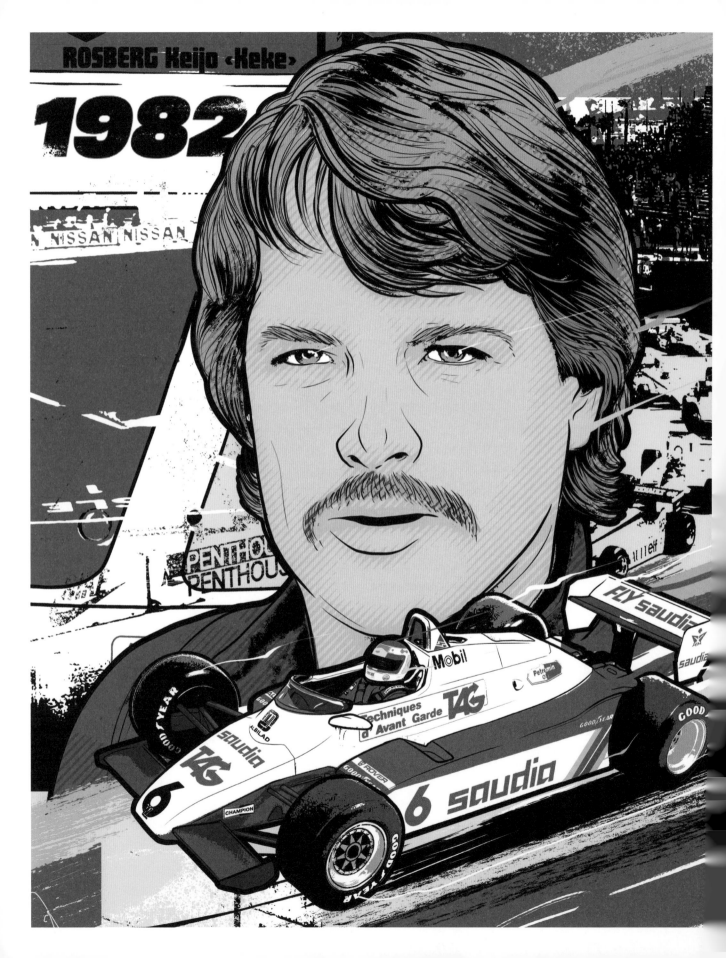

KEKE
ROSBERG

<< 1X CHAMPION >>

Born in Sweden and raised in Finland, Keke Rosberg might have looked like the bass player from a Eurovision disco-pop band, but his driving style was pure punk rock. Lurid, wild, at the absolute limit, taking every risk, he was the chain-smoking poster boy for racing on the edge. And while he may have won few Grands Prix in his career, there remain a great many Formula 1 drivers who won more races but never achieved the towering heights of the world championship. Rosberg was never anything but exhilarating—the perfect driver to bridge the divide from 1970s-era glam into a 1980s racing culture of brute force.

Keijo Erik Rosberg was born in 1948, and he had a taste for cars from before he could remember. He raced karts as a toddler and became a multiple Finnish, Scandinavian, and European champion. Despite his clear talent, however, recognition came late, winning in Formula Vee and Super Vee in his late twenties and making his Formula 1 debut after some Formula 2 runouts shortly before turning thirty. His early years in the sport were steady but unspectacular; he ran a succession of poor cars for teams that were either going nowhere or running out of money and time. By the 1981 season, it looked as though Rosberg, like the dogged teams he raced for, was destined to be a footnote in Formula 1 history. But when Alan Jones retired at the end of the season, Williams had an empty seat and a lack of options. It handed the drive to the only racer who'd shown promise and who was, most importantly, contractually available.

And so, despite never having won a Grand Prix in his life, Keke Rosberg lined up for Williams in 1982. The season was bookmarked by tragedy, but so too by a competitive convergence of the field that could have seen any one of six or more drivers take the crown. Rosberg won just a single race, his first in Formula 1, at the Swiss Grand Prix (which, ironically, was held in Dijon, France). But with consistently strong results across the season, and as his rivals took points off one another and struggled to match his consistency or his car's reliability, that one victory was all he needed. He was, quite incredibly, world champion.

As the turbo era began and Williams fell back from the front, Rosberg somehow stayed competitive by extracting superhuman times from cars that should not have been able to contend. When Williams finally got a turbo engine deal, Rosberg drove so fast he scared even himself, recording a 160-mph average at Silverstone, the fastest lap in F1 history at the time.

Although nobody but Rosberg knew it, 1986 would be his final year in Formula 1, and he chose to see out his career at McLaren. He only recorded one podium in that last season, but by then he'd had enough. He retired to focus on running junior series teams and manage the future generations of Finnish talent, including Mika Häkkinen and his own son, Nico Rosberg, both of whom would go on to be crowned Formula 1 World Champions.

ALAIN PROST

<< 4X CHAMPION >>

Although he discovered racing at the relatively advanced age of fourteen, Alain Prost became one of the sport's greatest champions, winning four Formula 1 World Championships. He was a technically gifted driver who never asked too much of his cars and combined tactical acumen with a graceful style. But his inability to play politics—born of an absolute refusal to accept any view other than his own—saw him ruffle more than a few feathers during his career.

Born in France in 1955, he was nearly twenty by the time he started competing seriously. As French karting champion in 1975, however, he won a paid season in Formula Renault. He won titles in that class before taking the crowns in both French and European Formula 3. Formula 1 teams were clamoring for his signature for 1980, and he signed with McLaren. The relationship was less than cordial, however, and after scoring a smattering of points, a combination of poor reliability, a lack of faith in his equipment, and disagreements with team management meant he broke away mid-contract to join Renault.

A French driver at a French team, Prost won his first race at the 1981 French Grand Prix. It should have been the start of something magical, but again, his relationship with the team soured. After three years he walked away and returned to a reinvigorated and much changed McLaren.

This was the start of Prost's era of brilliance. Over the next six seasons he won thirty Grands Prix and three world championships, cementing himself as one of the very best in the game. Then in 1988, he was partnered with the precociously

talented Brazilian Ayrton Senna, a relationship that began with admiration and ended in acrimony. Their driving styles were at odds, and so were their personalities. Senna won the championship during their first year as team-mates, a season in which McLaren won all but one race. In 1989, the duo were again the class of the field, but when Prost shut the door on his overtaking team-mate in Japan, the Frenchman was crowned champion in the most controversial of circumstances.

By then Prost had determined he could not work with Senna and left McLaren for Ferrari. But in 1990, despite their different teams, the duo again found themselves locked in a title fight and again wound up side by side in Japan. This time, it was Senna who failed to yield. This time, the Brazilian was named champion.

Prost was losing faith with Ferrari and was fired after publicly denouncing their cars. He sat out 1992 before making a remarkable comeback in 1993 for Williams, with whom he won his fourth and final world championship. When he retired at the end of 1993, his fifty-one race victories put him, at the time, at the top of the all-time list.

With his racing days done, Prost made peace with Senna and acted as a pallbearer at his great rival's funeral in 1994. Like many champions before, he tried his hand at team management, purchasing the French Ligier team, renaming it ProstGP, and later acting as an advisor for Renault's F1 aspirations—though perhaps more out of French pride than shrewd business acumen. Both projects were a failure and a sad final chapter to Prost's F1 story.

THE 1980S

135

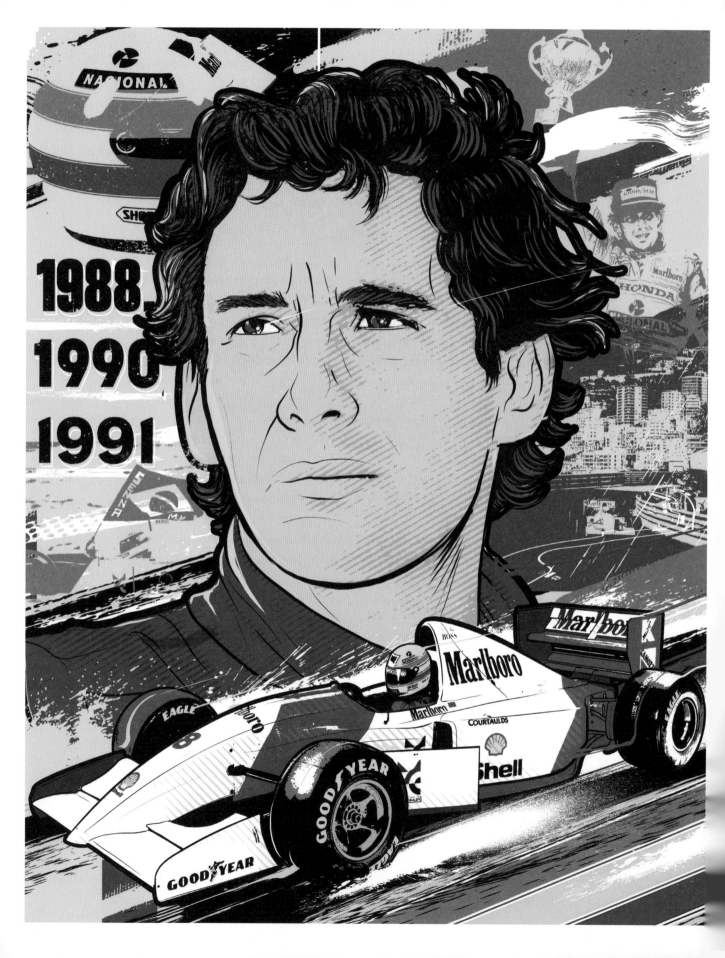

1988
1990
1991

AYRTON SENNA

« 3X CHAMPION »

Widely regarded as one of the greatest drivers who ever lived, Ayrton Senna was the master of his craft and a true artist, born of absolutely breathtaking ability. Like Jim Clark before him, even his rivals were aware that he was something genuinely special, which made his passing at the peak of his career so much harder to comprehend.

Born into a wealthy family in São Paulo, Brazil, in 1960, Senna didn't taste competition in karts until his teens, but his pace was immediate and his talent obvious. At twenty-one, he moved to England, where he forged a reputation for magnificent speed and terrifying risk-taking. He won three Formula Ford titles in his first two years, and the British Formula 3 championship in 1983.

By the time he arrived in Formula 1 the next season, the racing world was already talking about him, and he almost won the Monaco Grand Prix. He was signed by Lotus and took his first win in 1985. Three years brought him six wins, an astonishing sixteen pole positions, and, in 1987, third in the drivers' title race. In 1988 he sealed a dream move to McLaren.

It was here that Senna found his sweet spot. Feted by McLaren's team boss Ron Dennis, the love affair went both ways, as Ayrton adored the man and his team. He formed a tight bond with his engineers and mechanics, too. Such a closeness undoubtedly played a part in creating the animosity felt by his team-mate Alain Prost, but the two drivers were always destined to end up in conflict: both believed they were the best. The duo became bitter

rivals, making contact on track in determining the world championships in both 1989 and 1990.

His qualifying pace was otherworldly; his racecraft looked nigh on pre-ordained. Even Senna himself admitted to having out-of-body experiences in the car. By the end of 1993, he had won three world championships and was widely regarded as the best in the world. But as McLaren dropped off the pace, he moved to Williams, which had perfected the art of modern electronics. The season started poorly, however; Senna was left in the wake of Benetton and their young superstar Michael Schumacher.

At the third round of the season, pushing hard to stay in the lead of the race, Senna's car left the track and hit a wall. As his famous yellow helmet stayed silently still in the wreckage, the racing world had to come to terms with the unfathomable: Ayrton Senna was dead.

Brazil entered a period of national mourning, and more than three million people watched Senna's coffin carried through the streets of São Paulo. In Formula 1, the realization that the best in the world could still perish behind the wheel stunned the sport into immediate action, and its quest to improve safety has framed every key decision that has followed to this day.

Ayrton Senna is regarded as one of the greatest racing champions who ever lived. His six wins at Monaco remain the most at the sport's most-challenging track. To many, he remains one of the most gifted racing drivers of all time.

THE 1980S

GILLES VILLENEUVE

Like Ronnie Peterson, Gilles Villeneuve was a world champion in waiting. His bravery, racecraft, and absolute refusal to admit he was beaten made him both a beloved racer and surrogate son to Enzo Ferrari and a hero to fans the world over. But Villeneuve, like Peterson, not only never won the championship his talents deserved, but also tragically perished at the wheel.

Born in Quebec, Canada, in 1950, Gilles didn't take the normal route to Formula 1. His first successes came on snowmobiles. He was a fierce competitor on snow and ice, and when he tried his hand at single-seaters, the sideways style that became his calling card seemed a natural carryover from his roots in colder climes. Three Formula Atlantic titles proved he was more than a match for the circuit racers.

After impressing James Hunt at a Formula Atlantic race in 1976, Villeneuve made his F1 start for McLaren, but the British team decided not to pick him up full-time. Instead, Enzo Ferrari signed the Canadian to complete the 1977 season, and he made his full-time debut in 1978 for the Scuderia. It was a tough season, and the Italian press called for Villeneuve to be fired, but Enzo saw something special in him, and he was rewarded with Villeneuve's victory at the Canadian Grand Prix at the end of 1978.

In 1979, Villeneuve and new team-mate Jody Scheckter were the class of the field, and Villeneuve put in some of the performances for which he is most remembered, including his famous multi-lap side-by-side duel with René Arnoux at Dijon and his blast around the Zandvoort track in a Ferrari with a flat tire. Villeneuve was a loyal team player, and when asked to follow Scheckter home at Monza, he dutifully obliged to hand the South African the world championship. At the next race, Villeneuve went eleven seconds faster than anyone in practice, just to prove he was actually the quicker driver.

Ferrari's fortunes faded in 1980 and 1981 as the turbo era began and the Scuderia fell back. Yet Villeneuve was somehow able to overcome his car's shortcomings, pulling off victories that should have been impossible. His new team-mate Didier Pironi was left in his wake.

Villeneuve had the chance to race for McLaren in 1982 but opted to stay with Ferrari, and despite a tricky start to the year, he felt he had a competitive car. But at the San Marino Grand Prix, with Villeneuve leading a Ferrari one-two, Pironi ignored a team order to hold position and overtook him to win. Betrayed by his friend, Villenueve entered qualifying for the next race in Belgium, determined to beat his team-mate. On his final run, he was involved in an accident that launched his car into the air. As the Ferrari was torn apart, Villeneuve was thrown into the catch fencing at the side of the track, breaking his neck and severing his spinal cord. Gilles Villeneuve was dead at thirty-two.

His passing broke Enzo Ferrari's heart, and the Montreal track where he won his first Grand Prix was renamed for Canada's first Formula 1 hero. His name will forever be synonymous with bravery, loyalty, and staggering racing flair.

THE 1980S

139

BEST OF THE REST: 1980s

ELIO DE ANGELIS

A concert pianist who kept his fellow drivers entertained with virtuoso performances while they locked themselves into their hotels on various strikes in the 1980s, Elio de Angelis was a glorious racer and beloved member of the F1 paddock. Although he only won two Grands Prix in his career, his points tallies and raw pace when compared to those of his world champion team-mates Andretti, Mansell, and Senna prove just how good he really was. He was tragically killed during a test in France in 1986, never having fulfilled his tremendous potential.

JOHN WATSON

John Watson is probably better known these days as a commentator, but during the 1980s, the Northern Irishman was one of the toughest competitors in Formula 1. He made his debut in the 1970s, taking Penske's only F1 win in 1976, but his true form came to the fore in the early 1980s with McLaren. In the 1982 season, he finished third in the championship. In 1983, Watson set a record that still stands in Formula 1, winning in Long Beach from twenty-second on the grid—no driver has ever won from farther back.

DIDIER PIRONI, RENÉ ARNOUX, AND PATRICK TAMBAY

So filled with talent was the 1980s that it's necessary to bring three drivers together under one flag and one paragraph: Didier Pironi, René Arnoux, and Patrick Tambay. Along with Alain Prost, these men embodied France's wealth of incredibly gifted racers. Arnoux had beautiful car control and became the darling of both Renault and Ferrari, taking seven wins and twenty-two podiums. Tambay, too, had talent, which on his day was unbeatable, but he was such a lovely man he often lacked that ultimate punch. His second and final win was a beautiful one, at Ferrari's home track of Imola, driving the number 27 in which Gilles Villeneuve had been killed a year earlier. Pironi was a brilliant, good-looking, tough racer who won three Grands Prix. In the aftermath of Villeneuve's death, he, too, was involved in an accident; the Ferrari spared his life but destroyed his legs. His F1 career over, he took up powerboating but died in an accident in 1987.

DESIRÉ WILSON

Desiré Wilson is the only woman to have ever won a Formula 1 race, which she achieved at Brands Hatch in 1980 in the British Aurora AFX Formula One series. Although the race was not a sanctioned world championship event, her achievement was no less impressive when one considers the cars being raced and the competitive nature of the field at the time. She took seven other podiums in the championship and competed in IndyCar, sportscars, and at Le Mans.

TITANS OF THE 1980s

McLAREN

The 1980s began with the merger of McLaren and the Project 4 Formula 2 team, owned and run by former Brabham mechanic Ron Dennis. Dennis brought with him the brilliant designer John Barnard, whose McLaren MP4/1 proved revolutionary in its use of an entirely carbon-fiber monocoque chassis. With a TAG-branded Porsche turbo engine, McLaren leapt to the front of the sport in 1984, taking the constructors' title with twelve wins, as Niki Lauda beat McLaren team-mate Alain Prost to the drivers' crown by half a point. Prost won the title in 1985 and 1986, with McLaren again taking constructors' glory in 1985. In 1988, the team's fabled relationship with Honda began and Brazilian sensation Ayrton Senna was signed, creating a rivalry with Prost that defined the end of the decade. Senna and McLaren took the titles in 1988, winning fifteen of the sixteen races, then Prost and McLaren took the titles in 1989 with their new normally aspirated 3.5-liter Honda V10s. But after Senna and Prost's relationship soured, Prost left for Ferrari and took some of McLaren's top people, including Barnard, with him.

WILLIAMS

Williams

Frank Williams' eponymous squad began the 1980s as the team to beat, and for the next two decades Williams was always a threat for the world championship. Alan Jones got the ball rolling in 1980, taking the Drivers' Championship and helping the team take the Constructors' Championship, a feat the team repeated in 1981 even though their drivers were bested to the crown by Nelson Piquet. In 1982, one of the most open seasons in F1 history, Keke Rosberg, despite having failed to score a point in 1981, was crowned world champion in a Williams after winning just one race all year. A move from Ford to Honda signaled the start of a strong mid-1980s for Williams competitively, but the team was rocked when Frank was involved in a car accident that left him paralyzed. Frank remained in charge throughout his life, and in overcoming his injury, he became an even greater inspirational force. The team took the 1986 Constructors' Championship and both titles in 1987.

BRABHAM

With arguments swirling around the use of ground effect, Brabham used its final years of operation to maximum effect. The BT49, designed by Gordon Murray, took the team to multiple wins with Piquet. He won the 1981 drivers' title despite suspicions that the team was using illegal fuel—accusations over which Jean-Marie Balestre, despite his opposition to the FOCA teams, vehemently defended Brabham. With the ground effect era over, Brabham partnered with BMW to use their turbo engine, and in 1983, Piquet again delivered the drivers' crown in the brilliant BT52. Piquet won races in 1984 and 1985, but by now Brabham was falling behind its rivals. With Ecclestone more focused on his work with FOCA, Murray eventually left to join McLaren. When Brabham missed the deadline to enter the 1988 championship, it announced its withdrawal from the sport and was subsequently sold. Although it continued under various owners for a few years into the 1990s, the Brabham team was, for all intents and purposes, finished.

FERRARI

Although Ferrari took the Constructors' World Championships in 1982 and 1983, and took second in the Constructors' in 1984 and 1985, the 1980s were a horrible decade for the team. The death of Gilles Villeneuve and the career-ending accident of Didier Pironi in 1982 rocked Ferrari to its core. The turbo era didn't work out as well as Ferrari had hoped, and the team threatened to quit the sport and move to IndyCar if engine regulation changes didn't allow them to run V12s when the turbo era finally ended. Ferrari went as far as building an IndyCar, but it never raced, since a return to form in the late 1980s saw the team recommit to Formula 1. In 1988, at the age of ninety, Enzo Ferrari passed away. Less than a month later, at the Italian Grand Prix, Ferrari won their only race of the season, denying McLaren a perfect year of winning every race.

LOTUS

Despite being the first to construct an all-carbon-fiber F1 car, Lotus never raced their invention because its twin-chassis concept was banned. But that didn't deter the team of innovators from pushing the boundaries of what was achievable in the sport, and they became the first to experiment with active suspension. But team founder Colin Chapman's newest piece of genius would never be realized by the man himself—he died tragically of a heart attack at age fifty-two in 1982. Under the leadership of Peter Warr, and with designer Gérard Ducarouge and drivers such as Elio de Angelis, Nigel Mansell, and Ayrton Senna, Lotus found new success as their Renault-powered 94T—and its subsequent evolution to the 97T, 98T, and Honda-powered 99T—made the team a race winner again.

RENAULT

Having pioneered the turbocharged engine technology that defined the decade, Renault was perfectly placed to start the 1980s in the ascendency, and yet the French squad never quite achieved the levels of success they might have, as reliability issues saw them come unstuck. The team never finished higher than second in the Constructors' Championship, despite multiple brilliant and deserved race wins. As financial problems hit the parent company, Renault could no longer excuse the vast expense of running a factory team, and it withdrew at the end of the 1985 season to become solely an engine supplier.

BENETTON

The Benetton clothing company originally entered Formula 1 as a sponsor to the Alfa Romeo and Toleman teams, but when Toleman ran into financial difficulty, its sponsor bought the team. Their first season in 1986 saw Benetton use BMW engines and take pole positions and a victory for Gerhard Berger in Mexico. A switch to Ford in 1987 started with reliability issues but resulted in podiums. Benetton returned to the top step by the end of the decade and came third in the Constructors' Championship in 1988. At the end of 1989, Italian businessman Flavio Briatore was placed in charge of the team, and Nelson Piquet was signed to race for them.

RACE OF THE DECADE

1984 MONACO GRAND PRIX

Monte Carlo rarely provides thrilling races. Its narrow, unforgiving confines have always put overtaking at a premium and rarely supply the kind of swashbuckling duels that so often mark out the other "classic" Grand Prix tracks. But when one combines rain with this rabbit warren of a circuit, it can throw delightful curveballs. The 1972 Monaco Grand Prix was one such race, as was 1982—and 1996 was another absolutely wild affair. But it is 1984 that looms largest in the memory, thanks in no small part to the rivalry that grew between the drivers who finished on the top two steps of the podium that day.

Monaco is treacherous in the wet. Run on regular roads, the surface of the course is one of the most slippery of any track on the calendar, even in the dry. Factor in the painted road markings, which act like sheet ice in the wet, and the complete lack of runoff before cars find metal barriers at the edge of the circuit, and you have the perfect stage for carnage.

The 1984 race was held in torrential rain. Right from the get-go, there were retirements—the Renault duo of Derek Warwick and Patrick Tambay was eliminated at the very first corner. Nelson Piquet spun his Brabham and stalled fifteen laps in. Nigel Mansell slid into the barriers and damaged his rear wing so badly he had to retire one lap later. Even the great Niki Lauda spun out with brake issues in the monstrous deluge that faced the drivers that day.

Yet driving his McLaren MP4/2 out front, Alain Prost was almost perfect. He started from pole position and led—save for a few laps when Mansell nipped past—without much worry. As the race went on and conditions became steadily worse, however, his brakes started to go the way of team-mate Lauda's. Yet while Lauda spun and retired, Prost was able to keep going, but his lead was being cut each time over the line.

The driver hot on his heels was rookie sensation Ayrton Senna, driving for the unfavored Toleman team. In these conditions, the usual disparity between cars meant next to nothing, and Senna was pulling Prost in rapidly. The Brazilian would become known as a wet-weather specialist, but at this time he was still relatively unknown in Formula 1. Prost was feeling the heat. Each time past the pits he waved frantically to have the race stopped, and eventually he got his wish. The red flag was waved just as Senna had caught the McLaren in his sights.

Yet despite feeling he'd had the win taken from him, Senna had whacked his suspension into the barriers earlier in the race, and there's no telling if he'd have made the flag in a full-distance contest. What we do know is that the unsung hero that day was Stefan Bellof driving the even-less-regarded Tyrrell 012. Having qualified last, he was lapping faster than both Senna and Prost, and there's every chance it would have been he who might have triumphed had the race gone to conclusion. Sadly, we'll never know.

Bellof would never see the top step of the F1 podium his talent deserved—he was killed tragically one year later racing sportscars at Spa. As for Senna and Prost, the Monaco Grand Prix proved to be the prologue of their era-defining rivalry.

THE
199

BY 1994, FORMULA 1 HAD raced for more than a decade without a fatality at a race event, but all of that changed over the course of one of the sport's darkest weekends. The elimination of electronic driver aids at the start of the 1994 season created concern from a number of drivers that the powerful and now-skittish cars would be difficult to control. After a number of big accidents in testing, their fears appeared well-founded. Then, at the third race of the season in Imola, their worst fears were realized. On Friday, Rubens Barrichello was involved in a horrifying accident that left him hospitalized, and on Saturday, Austrian rookie Roland Ratzenberger crashed at the Villeneuve corner and was killed instantly.

On Sunday, the drivers, teams, and fans faced race day in a somber mood. Ayrton Senna, having moved from McLaren to Williams for the new season, placed an Austrian flag in his cockpit to raise at the end of the Grand Prix to salute Ratzenberger. But he never got the chance. The three-time champion, one of the greatest to ever grace the sport, crashed on the seventh lap and was declared dead on arrival at hospital. The shockwaves from Senna's passing changed the face of the sport forever.

Safety was high on the agenda from the start of the 1990s, with quick-release steering wheels made mandatory along with increasingly strict crash testing carried out on cars' survival cells, fuel tanks, and seat belts. Yet 1994's sudden ban on electronic aids coupled with the reintroduction of refueling seemed to signal a potential step backward. In the aftermath of the weekend at Imola, a pitlane speed limit was introduced, and almost thirty high-risk corners at various circuits were identified and amended with chicanes or removed altogether.

In the years that followed, engine capacity was cut to slow cars, cockpit regulations changed to raise the height and length of protection around the driver's helmet, and more ferocious impact testing was carried out on all the cars. Debris fencing around racetracks was improved, and the FIA took over the approval of all medical officers on site for F1 events, along with implementing faster and more representative safety cars, medical intervention vehicles, and the FIA medical car. Finally, at the end of the decade, the cars were made thinner, slick tires were mandated to run with grooves to slow them down, wheel tethers were introduced to stop errant wheels from becoming dislodged from cars in accidents, and flexible wings were banned.

Over the final six years of the decade, almost every major change in technical regulations occurred as a result of safety considerations, whether that was increasing the strength of the cars or in an attempt to control their speeds. Under the new leadership of Max Mosley, the FIA pushed to increase circuit safety along with car safety, and this influenced the road industry, as many Formula 1 safety developments found their way onto road vehicles. In the aftermath of Senna's death, the Grand Prix Drivers' Association was turned into a union of sorts, giving extra weight to the voices of the racers themselves. Many of the changes implemented were created not only through a close cooperation between the FIA and the teams but also in collaboration with the GPDA.

The decade had started with Ayrton Senna and Alain Prost as the drivers to beat, but the loss of Senna, coupled with Prost's retirement, paved the way for a new generation of racing superstars to come to the fore. Of them, Michael Schumacher and Mika Häkkinen were the two most notable, both taking two championships. Williams and McLaren remained on top, but Benetton emerged as a championship contender with Schumacher behind the wheel. The German driver and British team were never far from controversy, however. Suspicions linger to this day as to whether Benetton was somehow able to utilize banned electronic driver aids on their 1994 car, and Schumacher became embroiled in numerous on-track altercations with his rivals. His move to Ferrari after securing his second

drivers' title became one of the stories of the era, as he made it his mission to return the Scuderia to their first world championship in over a decade. Ferrari took the constructors' crown in 1999, rounding off the decade in superb form to establish the foundations upon which their next era of dominance in the sport would be built.

And as former great teams such as Lotus, Brabham, and Tyrrell slipped out of the sport with a whimper, new teams made their mark. The much-loved Jordan squad became firm fan favorites; Peter Sauber's Swiss team, while never race winners, made an impact; and two world champions, Sir Jackie Stewart and Alain Prost, launched their own outfits to varying levels of success. From a calendar perspective, the seasons stayed locked at around sixteen races, with Malaysia the most notable new addition. Also, starting in 1991, all points accumulated over the year counted toward the championship for the very first time, even if only the first six drivers across the line continued to score points.

While the decade was framed by tragedy, the 1990s brought a new fan base to the sport as its televised broadcasts continued to grow. Global awareness of the sport and modern-day superstars like Schumacher launched Formula 1 toward new heights. A new millennium stood ahead.

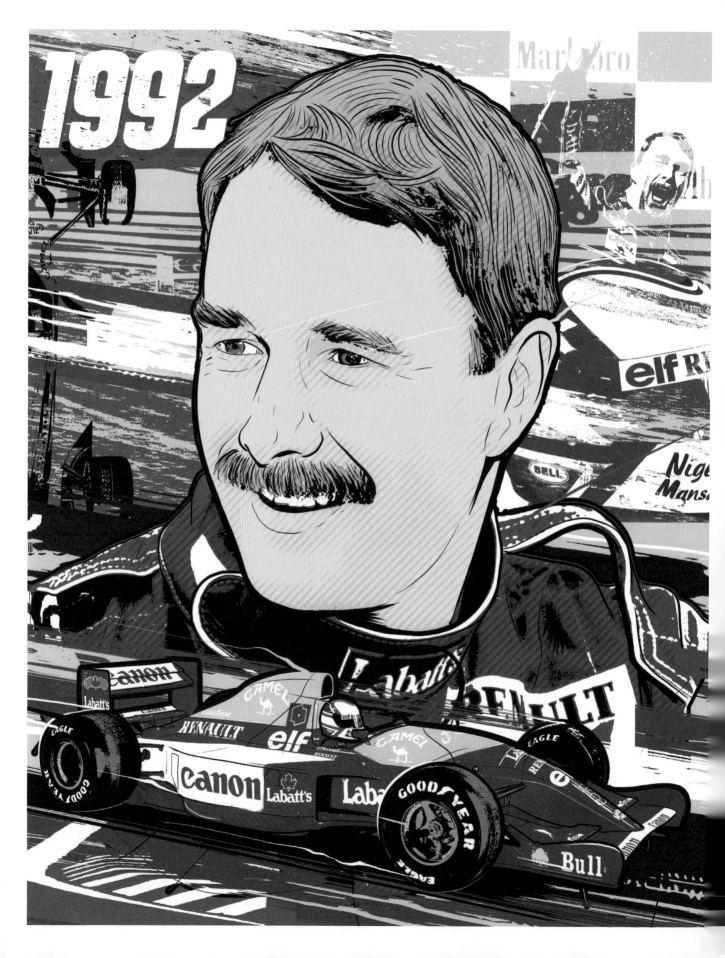

NIGEL MANSELL

《 1X CHAMPION 》

Nigel Mansell's Formula 1 career owed as much to his perseverance as it did to his speed. His driving style was all-out attack and absolute commitment. Yet despite his sometimes difficult personality, he was, often begrudgingly, loved by those he raced for. And the working man's fighting spirit of the mustachioed underdog in a flat cap made him a fan favorite the world over.

It's a miracle that Mansell, born near Birmingham, England, in 1953, ever made it to Formula 1 at all. He had neither money nor, it seemed, luck. He crashed often in his early career, the ferocity of his many accidents breaking both his neck and his back. He nevertheless dominated British Formula Ford in 1976 and 1977, but after patchy results in Formula 3, he needed someone with faith in him to give him a chance in Formula 1.

That man was Colin Chapman, who recruited Mansell as a test driver for his Lotus F1 team in 1980. Mansell aided the team in their car-development program so well that Chapman gave him a few race drives. During his F1 debut, a fuel leak caused Mansell to suffer first- and second-degree burns. Yet he raced through the pain until the car retired. He got a few more starts but made no real impact, and so it was a surprise when Chapman announced he'd be racing full-time in 1981.

Chapman's death left Mansell emotionally devastated and politically marginalized at the new Lotus, and with relationships at the team strained, he moved to Williams in 1985—but not before physically pushing his Lotus across the line after

it failed yards from home at the Dallas Grand Prix. He got his first wins with Williams driving what would become his lucky red five, and in 1986, he truly came of age, missing out on the title due only to an infamous tire blowout in the final race. He finished second again in 1987.

Mansell spent two years with Ferrari, but when the Italian powerhouse signed Alain Prost in 1990, Mansell announced he'd rather retire than partner the Frenchman. Only an offer from Williams kept him in the sport, and after a troubled 1991 season, everything came together with the all-conquering FW14B. In 1992, Mansell won nine of sixteen races to be crowned world champion. Yet no sooner had he celebrated his success than he announced he was leaving Formula 1 to race in IndyCar, furious that Williams had signed Prost for 1993.

Few believed Mansell would adapt well to the rigors of IndyCar, but he proved all doubters wrong to take the 1993 championship. When 1994 became a more complicated year, he was convinced to return to Formula 1 to aid his former Williams team members as they reeled from the death of Ayrton Senna. A win in the final race of the season showed he'd lost none of his determined speed.

Mansell signed to race for McLaren in 1995, but the car lacked pace and Mansell lacked motivation. The relationship ended after two miserable races, and that was the last that Mansell drove in the sport he'd conquered.

THE 1990S

151

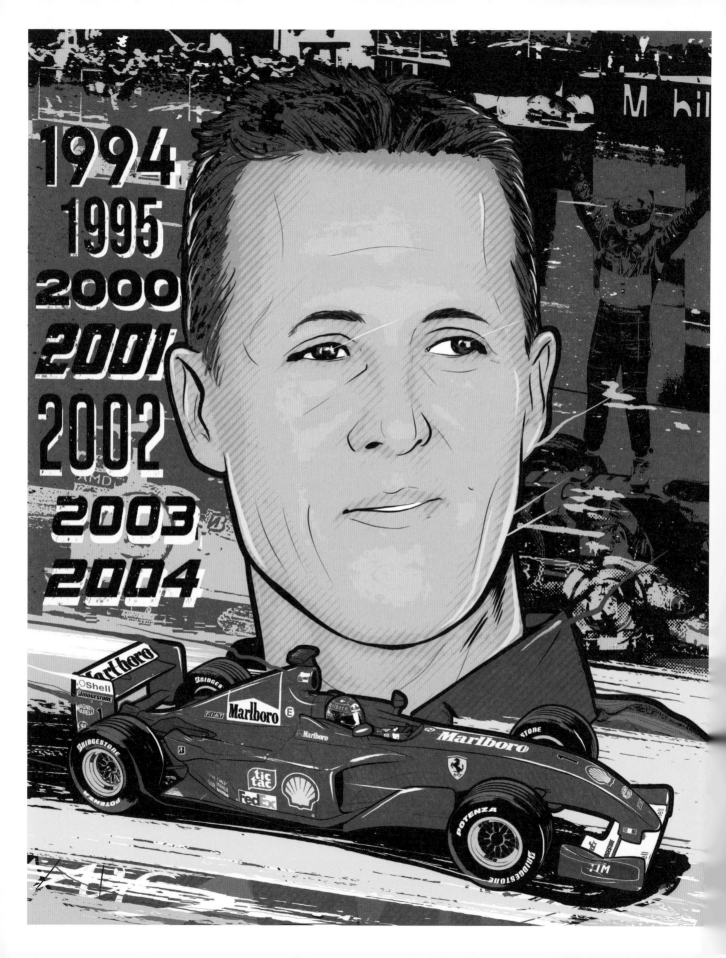

MICHAEL
SCHUMACHER

《 7X CHAMPION 》

A man who changed the face of Formula 1 by completely reinventing the way in which racers raced and teams worked, Michael Schumacher was a hero both in his native Germany and around the world, reinvigorating both Ferrari and Formula 1 and, in the process, becoming a global icon.

Born in 1969 near Cologne, he raced from a young age, and after winning German and European kart titles and German Formula 3, he progressed to racing sportscars with Mercedes. When F1 team boss Eddie Jordan needed a stand-in driver for the 1991 Belgian Grand Prix, the fast young German seemed a good prospect. Schumacher qualified a sensational seventh, and by the time of the next race, Benetton had stolen him and made him a full-time F1 driver. He won his first Grand Prix the very next year.

In 1994, a season-long battle with Williams driver Damon Hill set up a final race showdown. Schumacher left the track and hit a wall, and as Hill moved to take the lead, Schumacher closed the door and the duo made contact. With both Hill and Schumacher out of the race, Schumacher had his first, though controversial, world title.

In 1995, Schumacher and Benetton were unbeatable and the German became a two-time champion. But at the height of his powers, he joined Ferrari to help the team fight back to the front. He created magic. After a year of learning in 1996, the car and the team fought for the title in 1997. Again, he faced a Williams driver, again it went to the final race, and again Schumacher closed the door. This time, though, he lost the title and was disqualified from the entire season for deliberately trying to take his rival out. In 1999, a broken leg resulting from a crash at the British Grand Prix saw him sit out half the year.

His legend truly begins in 2000—he won every world championship for five consecutive seasons, victorious in forty-eight races. He and Ferrari were unstoppable. Never before had a driver been such a central part of a team, or so key to all decision-making. He worked tireless nights with engineers and oversaw the work his mechanics carried out, always searching for the smallest gain.

Schumacher shocked Formula 1 by announcing his retirement in 2006, but he returned in 2010 with Mercedes as the German manufacturer made their reappearance in the sport. But as with so many comebacks, Schumacher's didn't bring the successes of the past—he took just one podium in his final fifty-eight races, yet he had sown seeds at the team that blossomed after his second and final retirement.

Tragically, while on a skiing holiday at the end of 2013, Schumacher fell, suffering a devastating head injury. He has not been seen in public since, and little is known of his health today, other than that he lives with his family in Switzerland. One of the greatest drivers to ever grace Formula 1, Schumacher changed the face of the sport and set an astonishing record of success: 7 world championships, 155 podiums, 91 wins, 77 fastest laps, and 68 pole positions. To an entire generation, Michael Schumacher *is* Formula 1.

THE 1990S

153

DAMON HILL

《 1X CHAMPION 》

Damon Hill became the first racing driver in history to follow in the footsteps of his father to also reach the summit of Formula 1 and be crowned world champion. His ascent to the top was rooted in determination, hard work, and honoring his family name. He took on one of the sport's all-time greats and beat him to forever cement himself in the annals of F1 history, becoming one of the most popular drivers of his generation.

The son of two-time world champion Graham Hill, Damon was born in 1960, and he grew up surrounded by the world of racing. Family get-togethers were filled with a who's who of Formula 1. He was just fifteen years old when his father died in a plane accident, leaving him and his family distraught and taking away the financially comfortable existence they had always known.

Hill had to grow up fast, but the lure of racing was ever present. He began competing on two wheels at the age of twenty-one, using the same simple helmet his father had made famous, and soon he moved into single-seaters, where he showed promise but struggled to gain the financial backing or competitive opportunities to really shine. That didn't stop Frank Williams from seeing his potential, however, and Hill was signed as a test driver for the Williams F1 Team.

After making his Formula 1 debut for the then-uncompetitive Brabham team, his major break came in 1993 when he was promoted to race alongside Alain Prost at Williams. In a car he'd played a huge hand in developing, Hill won three races, and when his new team-mate Ayrton Senna was tragically killed in 1994, Hill was made the team leader at Williams after just twenty-one F1 races. He ran Michael Schumacher to within a point of the world championship in 1994, and finished as runner-up again in 1995.

In 1996, Hill proved mighty, contending with a fast new team-mate in IndyCar hotshot Jacques Villeneuve and winning half the Grands Prix that year to be crowned world champion. Incredibly, however, Williams had already decided not to renew his contract for 1997, and so the reigning champion found himself looking for scraps. He settled on the backmarker team Arrows, and while he never expected any level of success with them, he very nearly won the Hungarian Grand Prix.

For 1998, Hill moved to Eddie Jordan's much-loved eponymous team and helped them to their first Formula 1 victory at a soaking wet Belgian Grand Prix. But by 1999, his passion for the sport was waning, and he decided to walk away to spend more time with his family. Living in the real world gave him the first opportunity in his life to deal with the tragedies and hardships he'd experienced, and he fell into a depression rooted in the loss of his father and idol. His path through therapy brought an introspection and understanding that has made him one of the most fascinating and respected Formula 1 pundits of the modern era. Loved by all, Damon Hill carried on his father's legacy and added a final, beautiful chapter to the Hill family Formula 1 story.

THE 1990S

JACQUES VILLENEUVE

《 1X CHAMPION 》

As the son of one of the most legendary figures in motorsport, it seems only natural that Jacques Villeneuve should have followed in his father's footsteps. Yet Gilles Villenueve's death warned his son of the dangers inherent in the sport, and despite the opportunities open to Jacques due to his lineage, it was clear from early on that the young Villeneuve would do things his own way and for his own reasons. It was never about living up to expectations or stepping out of a shadow. Jacques Villeneuve raced because he could, never because he felt that he should.

Born in Quebec, Canada, in 1971, Villeneuve traveled with his father to races as a child. He showed interest in competing from a young age, but when his father was killed in 1982, Jacques' love of racing understandably diminished. Yet not forever. When the call of the track became overpowering, he raced with his mother's blessing. He showed promise and potential from the outset, but he was never what people expected him to be. Jacques had to work harder to perfect his art than his rivals, which he did through a variety of different disciplines, from saloon cars to sports-cars, Formula 3 and Formula Atlantic. In 1994, he graduated to IndyCar and took a win that very first year as a rookie, making an immediate impression with his hard driving style and blunt and outspoken approach to the media. In 1995, he won the Indy 500 en route to the championship.

By the 1990s, it was rare to see drivers move from IndyCar to Formula 1, but so impressed was the Williams team with what they'd seen that they signed the young champion to partner Damon Hill in 1996. He took pole on debut and very nearly won his very first F1 race.

Villeneuve had arrived and proved to be every bit as impressive as Williams had hoped. He ran Hill closely for the world championship, finishing second, and in 1997 he battled Michael Schumacher all the way to the final race, where he achieved what his father had not and was crowned Formula 1 World Champion.

Williams had a disappointing season in 1998, and in 1999 Villeneuve decided to leave the team to join a brand-new outfit, BAR (British American Racing), run by his manager. Despite showing flashes of brilliance, Villeneuve never took a win or even a podium during his five years at the team. By the end of 2003, it looked as though his time in the sport was over. But in 2004, he was given three races at Renault, which led to a full-season contract with Sauber in 2005. By mid-2006, with results still not coming, he walked away from Formula 1 in a sad end to what had started as the most promising of stints in the sport.

Life after F1 saw Villeneuve record and release an acoustic rock album, but he was never far away from racing. He ran NASCAR, stock cars in Brazil, and Formula E, and he races today at Le Mans, where he remains one of few drivers who can still win the fabled Triple Crown of Motorsport.

THE 1990S

MIKA HÄKKINEN

《 2X CHAMPION 》

One of the outright fastest drivers of the 1990s, Mika Häkkinen was a genuinely phenomenal talent who overcame tremendous odds to reach the pinnacle of Formula 1 and the world championship crown. Honest and loyal, he was a racer who was respected by everyone who competed against him and loved for his warm and playful personality. One of Michael Schumacher's great rivals, he was the driver the seven-time champion respected the most.

Häkkinen was born in Finland in 1968, and he was five when his parents took him karting for the first time. Although he crashed, he was hooked. His parents were by no means rich, but they saved all they could to buy him his first kart. He repaid them with multiple championships on his route up the karting ladder. His path to single-seaters was aided by his new manager, 1982 world champion Keke Rosberg, and he won various Formula Ford titles, was Formula Opel champion, and in 1990 won the British F3 crown.

In 1991, Häkkinen got the call up to Formula 1, where he made his debut for Lotus. The team was by now a shadow of the all-conquering squad of the 1960s and 1970s, and even qualifying sometimes proved to be a struggle. Yet his perseverance and natural talent meant that by 1993 he was much in demand, with Williams and Ligier both trying to sign him and Lotus determined not to let him go. Despite numerous public arguments and legal fights, none of them won his services. Instead, McLaren swooped in and got their man.

Häkkinen began life at McLaren as a test driver, but when Michael Andretti, son of the great Mario, quit the team midseason, Mika got his chance. He outqualified the great Ayrton Senna in his first McLaren race and took a podium in his second. He led the team through difficult stretches in 1994 and 1995 to record eight podium finishes. But an accident after a tire failure at the 1995 season finale in Australia almost cost him his life. He made an incredible recovery and was back on the podium trail in 1996. He won his first Grand Prix in 1997.

The win set Häkkinen up perfectly for the start of 1998, and with eight wins, he was crowned world champion ahead of Ferrari's Schumacher. With five wins in 1999, Häkkinen made it back-to-back world championships. Going for his third title in 2000, he pulled off one of the greatest overtakes of all time on Schumacher at Spa as the rivals lapped Ricardo Zonta, but even at the peak of his powers, the combination of Schumacher and Ferrari proved too much for Häkkinen, and he had to settle for second in the world title fight.

His last season in Formula 1 was in 2001. His motivation and determination were drained after three title fights, and as his family grew, he felt an increasing fear of accidents. He announced a sabbatical for 2002 and took a final race win at the 2001 US Grand Prix. Häkkinen's sabbatical morphed into retirement, and although he went on to contest three seasons in the DTM, he never raced in F1 again.

THE 1990S

JEAN ALESI

There are drivers who have won more Grands Prix, who have finished higher in the world championship, and who have come far closer to taking the absolute prize in Formula 1 than Jean Alesi, but few have possessed his raw talent and ability. Had circumstances worked out differently, there's every chance the emotional and well-loved French Sicilian might have ruled Formula 1 on multiple occasions.

Born in 1964, Alesi didn't start karting until the relatively late age of sixteen, but by 1983 he'd moved into cars, by 1987 he'd won the French F3 championship, and in 1989 he took the crown in Formula 3000. His promotion to Formula 1 came, by chance, at Tyrrell in that same 1989 season. After contractual clashes meant a seat suddenly became available, the team opted to take a chance on the man leading F1's feeder series at the time. Alesi ran as high as second and finished his debut Grand Prix fourth. He was given an immediate eighteen-month contract and continued to race in Formula 1 alongside his F3000 commitments, as he ran to the junior title.

His first full season in Formula 1 was in 1990, but with half a year under his belt and a rookie team-mate, he was already the team's most experienced racer. He began the season with a bang. At the very first race, he led for twenty-five laps, holding the far faster McLaren of Ayrton Senna behind him while dueling with the legendary champion. Alesi came home second and repeated the result in Monaco. By the middle of the 1990 season, almost every top team wanted Alesi to race for them the next year, and he had a decision to make.

Alesi chose to race for Williams and signed a deal, but after it delayed announcing him, he grew suspicious of the team's intentions. Attracted in no small measure because of his part-Italian heritage, Alesi was eventually lured away by Ferrari. But as Williams went on a run of championships, Ferrari endured lean years. He raced in red for five seasons, taking on the number 27 car, which meant so much to the Scuderia's fans due to its long association with greats like Gilles Villeneuve. But in all that time, he won just one race due to a combination of poor luck and poor cars. He continued in Formula 1 until 2001, but that single win remained the highlight of a career that promised so much more.

How different might things have been if he'd just stuck to the Williams deal? In 1991 and 1992, the Williams FW14 and 14B ended up being the class of the field, and with Alesi at his early nineties best—considered by many to have been a younger and even more potent version of Nigel Mansell—there's every reason to think he might have taken at least one world championship before 1994, and quite possibly two or more.

As it was, Alesi followed his heart and in turn won not the races and titles his talent merited but the popularity and adoration his personality deserved.

THE 1990S

161

GERHARD BERGER

Amassing ten wins and forty-eight podiums, Gerhard Berger is best remembered for his tenures at McLaren and Ferrari, where he was adored by the teams and their fans. His Formula 1 career lasted throughout the 1980s and the majority of the 1990s. While never quite able to pull it all together for a tilt at the title, he was well-regarded and finished third in the championship twice. His friendship with Ayrton Senna was one of the closest between drivers in the sport in the nineties, and it led to hilarious stories of pranks being played, sometimes on the other drivers, but most often on each other.

RICCARDO PATRESE

Riccardo Patrese made his Grand Prix debut in 1977 and raced consistently through the end of the seventies and the whole of the eighties. However, it was as the decade ended and moved into the nineties where he found his richest form. He took third in the championships in 1989 and 1991, and in 1992—as Nigel Mansell's team-mate—he had his best F1 season, finishing second. The first F1 driver to start both 200 and 250 races, he took six wins and retired in 1993 as a much-loved member of the paddock.

HEINZ-HARALD FRENTZEN

A contemporary of Michael Schumacher, Heinz-Harald Frentzen was part of the same Mercedes program that launched the seven-time champion's career. He impressed many when he arrived in Formula 1 in 1994 with Sauber. Williams signed the German to replace Damon Hill for 1997, and he finished second in the championship that year. But his true season of seasons was 1999 when he moved to the small Jordan team. Against the much more favored Ferrari and McLaren drivers, he stayed in the title fight all season long, finishing third.

EDDIE IRVINE

Eddie Irvine announced his arrival in Formula 1 by overtaking Ayrton Senna to unlap himself. The Brazilian was so incensed that he punched the Northern Irishman. Seen as something of a party boy, Irvine lived a life of excess, but on his day, he could compete with the very best. He was signed to partner Michael Schumacher at Ferrari from 1996, and when the German was sidelined for much of 1999 with a broken leg, Irvine took his chance, winning four Grands Prix and narrowly missing out on the title.

GIOVANNA AMATI

Born into wealth, Italian Giovanna Amati was kidnapped as a teenager and held in a wooden cage for almost three months until her parents were able to pay her ransom. But her mental fortitude and incredible self-belief allowed her to move past this harrowing experience, follow her dreams, and rise through the ranks of motorsport, winning races and eventually making it all the way to Formula 1. Although she failed to qualify for the three race weekends she entered with Brabham in 1992, her replacement, Damon Hill, needed six races to get the same car into a race. Her story remains one of incredible resilience and determination, and she is the last female driver to attempt to qualify for a Grand Prix.

TITANS OF THE 1990s

WILLIAMS

The 1990s belonged to Williams. With five championships, the British team proved to be the force against which all others were judged. Under Frank Williams and Patrick Head's guiding hands, design legend Adrian Newey led a technical department that consistently raised the bar. In the early years of the decade, the team also employed the brilliant mind of Paddy Lowe, who in 1992 mastered the art of electronics and active suspension with the all-conquering FW14B. Williams won four drivers' titles and ran to the constructors' crown in 1992, 1993, 1994, 1996, and 1997. But, as is often the case with successful teams, it eventually saw its most talented members lured away. The team thus ended the decade far beneath the championship pedigree it had held just a few years earlier.

McLAREN

McLaren started and ended the decade in the ascendency, but a string of changes of engine partner held the team in a state of flux in the middle of the decade. It had all started so well, as their partnership with Honda and lead driver Ayrton Senna took back-to-back titles in 1990 and 1991. A change in engine provider to Ford in 1993 (after Honda withdrew from the sport) resulted in five wins, but with Williams still dominant, Senna opted to leave at season's end to race for the reigning champions. The Ford deal lasted just a year before McLaren switched to Peugeot engines, again for just one year. In 1995, the team linked up with Mercedes, and when designer Adrian Newey joined from Williams, everything finally meshed. By the end of 1997, the team was finally competitive again, and in 1998 Mika Häkkinen and McLaren were world champions. Häkkinen repeated the feat in 1999, but by now Ferrari was on the march and snatched away the decade's final team crown.

BENETTON

Once Flavio Briatore took over the Benetton team, its rise to the top was swift. The Italian businessman was never universally loved in Formula 1 circles—many found him brash, and they distrusted him as an outsider—but he knew how to get the job done. He assembled a brilliant team that took on the establishment and won. By the end of Briatore's first season in 1990, the team finished third in the Constructors' Championship with three wins. When 1991 proved less successful, Briatore convinced Ross Brawn to join as technical director, and he developed incredible cars and exceptional race strategies. Together with Michael Schumacher, the team won races before launching an assault on the world championship in 1994. While unproven speculation still suggests the B194 car carried over illegal traction control, and despite being banned from two races and disqualified from two others, Schumacher took the crown. In 1995, Benetton added the Constructors' Championship to Schumacher's second drivers' title. Schumacher left for Ferrari with Brawn and chief designer Rory Byrne at the end of the year, and Benetton never regained the same form. Briatore was removed, and by the end of the decade, Benetton had slipped to only an occasional points scorer.

FERRARI

The Scuderia started the 1990s fighting for the title with Alain Prost losing out to Ayrton Senna in the final race of the season, but as McLaren and Williams pushed into the ascendency, Prost fell out with the team and was fired. The team slipped backward until, in 1993, former Peugeot rally boss Jean Todt was brought in to steady the ship. He started a long period of restructuring, creating an invisible barrier between the boardroom and the race team and hiring competent department heads to manage their own affairs, allowing him to take a wider view of the team and pull back from the micromanagement that had held it back. In 1996, Todt lured Schumacher away from Benetton, and with him Ross Brawn and Rory Byrne. This dream team, each cemented and confident in their roles, formed an almost unbeatable package, and Schumacher again fought for the title in 1997. While a broken leg ruled him out for much of 1999, Schumacher returned to help Ferrari take that year's Constructors' Championship. But the team's best years lay ahead in the 2000s.

JORDAN

Eddie Jordan had enjoyed a brief career as a racing driver before starting his own successful F3 team in the 1980s, and in 1991, he made the step up to Formula 1. The Gary Anderson–designed Jordan 191 is often considered the best-looking Grand Prix car of the era, one of the most beautiful of all time, and with it the team made an immediate mark. It took Jordan until 1994 to take their first pole and podium, but by the second half of the decade the team was a regular threat to the established order. They took their first win in 1998, and in 1999, Heinz-Harald Frentzen took two victories and found himself in the midst of the Drivers' Championship fight. The little team based at Silverstone never had the budget to be one of the major players, but led by one of the most enigmatic men in the sport, it won fans around the world.

LIGIER

In 1976, former French rugby player Guy Ligier bought the assets of the Matra team and began his own F1 enterprise. The team won multiple races in the 1980s before going through a difficult period at the end of the decade, but in the early 1990s, from 1992 into 1993, it had a sudden return to form. The team carried on to 1996, when Oliver Panis won one of the most memorable Monaco Grands Prix ever held. At the end of the season, Ligier was sold to Alain Prost, becoming Prost Grand Prix in 1997. By the end of its tenure in Formula 1, Ligier had won nine races and scored fifty podiums.

STEWART

Stewart Grand Prix competed in just three Formula 1 seasons, but in that time it took five podiums and one Grand Prix win. Sir Jackie Stewart's son, Paul, had been running his own F3 team for some time, but in 1997, he joined forces with his father and partnered with Ford to move into Formula 1. They scored a podium in their debut season. After a difficult 1998, they returned in 1999 with regular points and three podiums for Rubens Barrichello and a win for Johnny Herbert at the Nürburgring. The team sold up to Ford at the end of the year to be rebranded as Jaguar, which itself was eventually sold to Dietrich Mateschitz to form Red Bull Racing.

EUROPEAN GRAND PRIX

1993

DONINGTON

RACE OF THE DECADE

1993 EUROPEAN GRAND PRIX

In the 1990s and 2000s, the European Grand Prix was the name given to a race that shifted location around the continent on an almost-annual basis. In 1993, the honor fell to Britain and Donington Park, a tricky little track with few genuine overtaking opportunities. But the combination of the typically changeable British weather and an inspired drive from Ayrton Senna has made this race consistently touted as one of the greatest of all time—not because it presented a wide open battle for the win, but because it so exemplified the peerless perfection of a masterful champion at the peak of their powers.

In the height of the era of electronic driver aids, McLaren found themselves lagging behind. With an unfavored Ford engine and against the might of the Williams-Renault package, Senna nevertheless took McLaren to multiple race wins in 1993. But such was the serenity of his dominance on that wet bank-holiday weekend in May that few of Senna's career drives are remembered as fondly.

He started the race from fourth place, having qualified over one and a half seconds behind longtime rival Alain Prost in a Williams, and as the race got under way on a sodden track, Senna fell to fifth behind the two Williamses, Karl Wendlinger's Sauber, and Michael Schumacher's Benetton. Yet by the end of that first lap, he was leading, deftly passing Schumacher, then dispatching Wendlinger with a sumptuous move around the outside. He eased past the Williams of Damon Hill, then nipped up the inside of Prost such that as he started the second lap, all that appeared in his mirrors was spray.

Senna switched to slick tires on the eighteenth lap, his first of five stops that saw him call conditions perfectly as the intermittent rain came and went. The Williams team, by contrast, was at sea. Hill stopped six times and was the only driver to finish on the same lap as Senna. Prost stopped seven times. But as Williams scrambled, other drivers shone. Rubens Barrichello at one point raced as high as second in his Jordan and looked set to finish a magnificent fourth until his car gave up on the seventy-first lap. Into his place stepped Johnny Herbert for the now-struggling Lotus team, his skill set making up for his meager equipment as he held on to slick tires even through the return of the rain. He finished fourth after starting eleventh. Riccardo Patrese and Fabrizio Barbazza completed the points positions, the latter scoring his first F1 point for the tiny Minardi team.

But the day belonged to Senna. Sure, he had traction control to help him in the conditions, but such was his peerless display of car control and his ability to call the conditions, to make the right choices, and to push on relentlessly on slicks in the wet that at times it appeared as though he was driving in a different formula. While Senna himself held other Grands Prix higher in his own personal list of greatest drives, for the Formula 1 fan base, it is Donington 1993 that is so often held up as his greatest, career-defining moment. He was untouchable from start to finish. Quite simply, nobody else stood a chance.

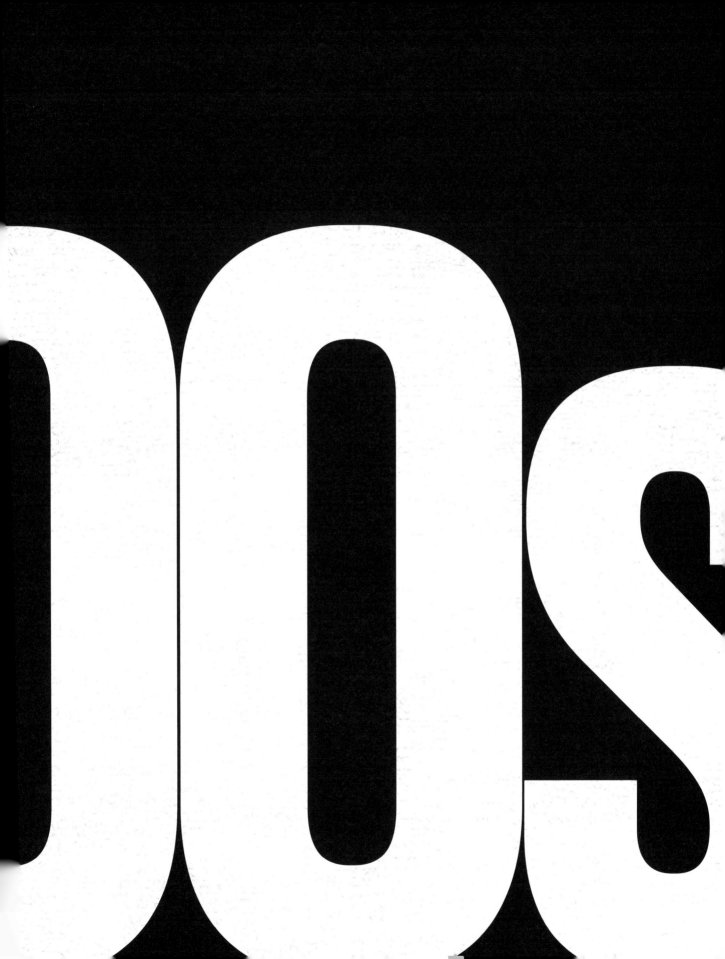

THE 2000S SAW FORMULA 1'S

star shine ever brighter as the sport expanded into new territories with new races and new teams. The major motor manufacturers all saw the potential of being involved in Formula 1, and while some chose to partner with existing independent teams, some entered on their own. A spending war erupted as the manufacturers threw unlimited funds at development, and the championship went for almost the entire decade without an independent team winning the title . . . until 2009, when the decade ended in an almost unbelievable fairy tale.

The early years of the decade were painted red or, to be more precise, rosso corsa. Ferrari ruled the early 2000s in a way not previously seen in Formula 1 history. So mighty was the team assembled by Jean Todt at the Scuderia that in the first five years of the era, Ferrari won fifty-seven of the eighty-five races run. Michael Schumacher won five consecutive world championships. Ferrari, including the 1999 win, took six titles on the bounce. Essentially, if you raced in Formula 1 between 2000 and 2004, and you weren't Michael Schumacher or Ferrari, you didn't stand a chance.

Yet a third of the race wins in that period went to other teams and drivers. McLaren was a consistent threat. Williams, too, with IndyCar convert Juan Pablo Montoya, had the runaway Schumacher train occasionally scared. Even Michael Schumacher's younger brother Ralf got in on the action as a regular race winner. From 2003, the top eight drivers in the sport started scoring points at the flag.

BMW returned to the Formula 1 fray, first partnering Williams and then as a team in its own right by taking over the Sauber outfit. Toyota entered the sport in 2002, and in 2006 Honda took over the BAR team, which had joined F1 at the turn of the decade to huge fanfare. Benetton was eventually taken over by engine provider Renault, marking the French manufacturer's return to the sport as a constructor, led by the homecoming of Flavio Briatore and his young charge Fernando Alonso, who finally toppled the Ferrari monopoly and took back-to-back titles in 2005 and 2006.

With heavy investment from Mercedes, McLaren swung back in the latter half of the decade, taking the fight to Renault and Ferrari in 2007, with their own young superstar Sir Lewis Hamilton lining up alongside the now-double-champion Alonso. But controversy overtook the season's narrative as the team was found guilty of accepting a dossier filled with secret Ferrari designs. McLaren's drivers missed out on the title by a point, and the team itself was fined $100 million and stripped of all its points. Meanwhile, Ferrari rediscovered its form to grab the title with McLaren's own protégé, Kimi Räikkönen, who had moved to the Scuderia that same year to replace the now-retired Michael Schumacher. McLaren and Hamilton made amends the following year, denying Ferrari's Felipe Massa the title on the last corner of the last lap of the last race of the 2008 season, even if Ferrari themselves took what would end up being their last Constructors' Championship to this day.

From a regulatory perspective, the 2000s were an interesting period. The FIA admitted it couldn't police the use of traction control, and so the organization had to legalize it in 2001—they later standardized electronic control units in 2008 to stamp out traction control once and for all. As costs rose out of the reaches of the smaller teams, engines were limited to one per weekend to try to pull expenditures back; grid drops were introduced for the first time for those who went over their allocation. Engine development was halted by freezing specifications in a further attempt at easing costs. The financial burden became a particularly sore point when the engine regulations changed, forcing all teams to shift from V10 to V8 engines. To appease the smaller teams, they were allowed to run detuned V10s to save money and improve reliability in the early years of the new engine rules.

From a safety perspective, one of the biggest changes in the 2000s was the introduction of head and neck support (HANS), a safety device designed to limit the movement of a driver's helmet and head in the event of an accident and so limit potential brain and spinal injury. And slick tires were no longer slick. For the first time since 1970, dry-weather tires featured grooves in an attempt to limit grip and slow speeds.

Aerodynamic development advanced almost unchecked. From the middle of the 2000s, an increasing number of flicks and wings appeared at almost every conceivable location on the cars in an attempt to pull in every scrap of downforce possible. And in 2007, when Formula 1 was left with just one tire supplier, the rules were amended to ensure that all drivers had to run both hard and soft compound tires in a Grand Prix. But the cars underwent huge changes in 2009, when the technical regulations were rewritten. The aero appendages were banned, rear wings were made tall and narrow, and front wings became low and wide as slick tires returned. The engines were limited to 18,000 rpm, and for the first time, teams could harness and reuse power created under braking using the kinetic energy recovery system (KERS).

By the end of the decade, years of fruitless and low-key results for some of the major manufacturers forced them to rethink their race programs. At the end of 2008, Honda suddenly and unexpectedly withdrew, despite having put a huge investment into the new rules package for 2009. Ross Brawn, then team principal for the Japanese squad, bought the team's entry for one pound, secured an engine supply from Mercedes, and employed all the Honda F1 staff at what was now his own team, Brawn GP. In its one and only season in Formula 1, Ross Brawn's team did the unthinkable: it took pole and won on debut, and by season's end, Jenson Button, driving a Brawn, was world champion. Brawn also won the Constructors' Championship. Toyota and BMW followed Honda's lead and pulled out, as global financial pressure led to all major manufacturers reconsidering their position in the sport. From a decade of factory dominance, the 2010s would begin with independents again in the ascendency.

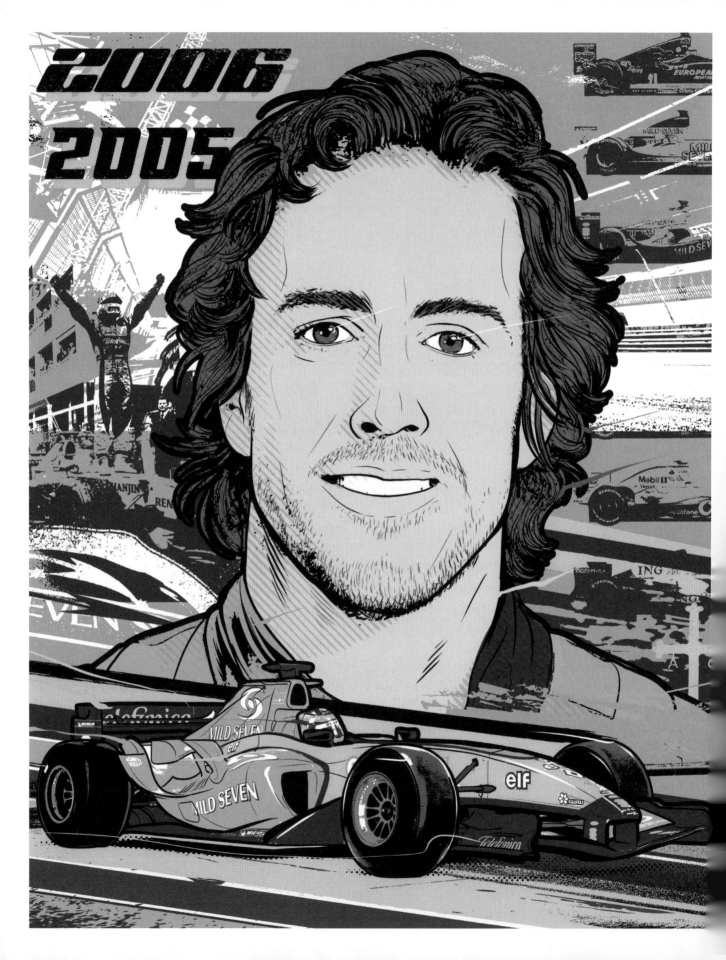

FERNANDO ALONSO

« 2X CHAMPION »

At the time of his first Formula 1 win, Fernando Alonso was the youngest Grand Prix winner in history. His ascent to the top ended Michael Schumacher's era of dominance, but after two years of taking the sport by storm, controversies and misguided moves put him increasingly far away from a third crown. But after leaving Formula 1, the lure was too strong, and at age forty, Alonso found himself back in the game.

Born in Oviedo, Spain, in 1981, Alonso got his first taste of racing in a homemade kart his father had built for his sister. It was young Fernando, however, who took to the thrill of speed, and by the age of five, he held a kart license. He progressed quickly, winning kart races and championships before embarking in single-seaters at seventeen, winning the championship in Formula Nissan at his first attempt and moving to Formula 3000. In 2001, at the age of nineteen, Alonso made his Formula 1 debut for back-of-the-grid team Minardi. Despite not scoring a point, he impressed the paddock with his pace and commitment. Now managed by Renault boss Flavio Briatore, Alonso spent 2002 as tester at the French team before stepping up to a full-time seat in 2003. He took four podiums and his first win that season, and four more podiums in 2004, which set him up for the biggest year of his career—2005.

He dominated the championship, winning seven races, and he repeated the feat with the same number of wins in 2006. His racecraft was masterful, making him one of the most fearless and naturally gifted drivers of his generation. But his struggles to play the complex game of Formula 1 politics would become a thorn in his side. As a two-time champion, he moved to McLaren for 2007, but once there, he discovered his rookie team-mate, Sir Lewis Hamilton, to be more of a handful than he'd expected. After only a year at McLaren, Alonso returned to Renault.

Two years with the French team brought little success until a move to Ferrari promised the chance of championships once again. Over the course of the next five years, he finished second in the championship three times before he and the team lost patience with each other. He managed to secure a shock move back to McLaren, but with the team nowhere near its former glories, he once again grew frustrated.

At the end of 2018, Alonso quit Formula 1 to compete in the World Endurance Championship with Toyota, which he won along with the 24 Hours of Le Mans. He competed at the Dakar Rally and attempted to complete the triple crown by contesting the Indy 500. Then out of the blue, he returned to Formula 1 in 2021. After two seasons back at his former Renault team (which had been rebranded as Alpine), he signed for Aston Martin, and in 2023, at the age of forty-one, now mellowed with age, he found himself regularly back on the podium, exhibiting the same staggering racecraft that had marked him out two decades before.

Now F1's most experienced racer in history, there's no telling how much longer Alonso will continue in the sport nor how much he might yet go on to achieve. There's seemingly no end in sight for the ever-competitive world champion.

THE 2000S

KIMI RÄIKKÖNEN

《 1X CHAMPION 》

A prodigy who showed incredible potential at such a young age that he made his Formula 1 debut on a provisional license, Kimi Räikkönen was a phenomenon. Fascinating and frustrating in equal measure, there were occasions where the world stood at his feet, but moments where it looked as if, despite his seemingly limitless talent, he'd never quite fulfill his destiny. Yet he did, being crowned world champion for the most famous team in the sport.

Born near Helsinki, Finland, in 1979, Räikkönen began his love affair with speed on mini-motocross bikes at age three. Soon he was showing tremendous promise on four wheels, racing karts from age ten. At eighteen he moved into single-seaters, which coincided with his compulsory military service, but he nevertheless managed to continue to compete. He eventually moved on to Formula Renault, where he contested twenty races, winning thirteen and taking two titles.

He impressed at a Formula 1 test with Sauber, and in 2001, having run just twenty-three races in open-wheel racing, Räikkönen was given his Grand Prix debut with a contract for the team. He was famously found asleep thirty minutes before the race began, but he scored points on debut. His solid performances caught the attention of McLaren, which brought him in to replace compatriot Mika Häkkinen in 2002.

A man of few words who notoriously detested media appearances, Räikkönen quickly became a fan favorite. He did things his own way and raced the way he acted, straightforwardly and with absolute conviction. His radio calls became the stuff of legend, as he gave short shrift to any orders he didn't agree with. Although seen as taciturn and moody, he knew how to have fun and made sure to do so at every opportunity.

The move to McLaren turned Räikkönen into a multiple-race winner, but the championship eluded him throughout five years at the team. This period coincided with Michael Schumacher and Ferrari's era of domination and the emergence of Alonso and Renault in the mid-2000s. Yet his reputation as a champion in waiting saw him sign for Ferrari for 2007 to replace the outgoing Schumacher. Arriving at the final race of the season, he had won five races to each McLaren driver's four apiece, and a brilliant final drive and sixth victory netted him the world championship by a single point. He won further races, but by the end of 2009, his star had begun to dim, and he walked away from the sport to contest rallies and NASCAR.

As with so many, the pull of Formula 1 proved too strong, and he returned to rejuvenate the Lotus/Renault team before sensationally returning to Ferrari, where he stayed for another five seasons. Although he was never quite the Räikkönen of old, his consistency and relaxed nature made him a perfect team-mate for the Scuderia's lead drivers. For his two final seasons, he returned to Sauber, now renamed Alfa Romeo, and retired at the team where it had all begun. He remained, up to his last race in 2021, one of the most naturally quick racers in the sport. He remains Ferrari's last world champion.

THE 2000S

SIR LEWIS HAMILTON

《 7X CHAMPION 》

From humble beginnings, Sir Lewis Hamilton rose through the motorsport ranks to place himself as one of the all-time greats. He didn't just define his generation, he redefined what a world champion could be, melding the most incredible car control and outrageous speed with a wider awareness of how to use his fame to further causes close his heart. A legend on the track, Hamilton has become a global icon over the course of his career.

Hamilton was born in Stevenage, England, in 1985. His parents separated when he was two, and at twelve, he went to live with his father, who worked three jobs to be able to afford to send his son karting. At an awards ceremony at the age of thirteen, he approached McLaren boss Ron Dennis to tell him he'd like to race for him one day. Impressed with the youngster's attitude, Dennis and McLaren started to financially back Hamilton's career. He repaid them with European and world karting titles before graduating to single-seaters and taking Formula Renault, Formula 3, and GP2 championships. He signed to race for McLaren in Formula 1 for the 2007 season.

He got a podium on debut, and his first victory in just his sixth start. Despite his inexperience, he was able to match (and often defeat) his two-time champion team-mate Fernando Alonso, who didn't take kindly to being shown up. Hamilton missed the title in his rookie season by a single point, but he made good in his second year to be crowned 2008 world champion. The manner in which he did so—making a crucial pass on the last corner of the last lap of the last race to secure the points he required—reflected his resolve.

But McLaren began a steady decline. Hamilton won races every season, but after four years of failing to win another title, he took a gamble and left the team that had backed his entire career. His move to Mercedes proved to be the best decision of his life. There, partnered with childhood friend and karting team-mate Nico Rosberg, he was the focal point of an emerging powerhouse. The team started winning races and focusing on championships, but as their speed increased, Hamilton and Rosberg's relationship fractured. Rosberg won one title, but Hamilton won a further six, defeating all who tried to take his crown. He set new records for most poles, most wins, and most fastest laps.

But alongside his racing, Hamilton realized he had a wider role to play. As a prominent Black man in the predominantly white world of racing, he reckoned with the additional hurdles he'd been forced to overcome in his career. Not many people in his sport looked like him or had traveled his path. He was determined to use his position to push for change and make meaningful steps toward improving inclusion and equity in motorsport.

He shocked the world by announcing that he would race for Ferrari from 2025.

The partnership of the most successful driver in F1 history racing for the sport's most successful team is tantalizing.

JENSON BUTTON

《 1X CHAMPION 》

Many drivers have never found themselves with the right car at the right time, and even when they have, fewer still have been able to put everything together to win the greatest prize in motorsport. Jenson Button had one golden year, one opportunity to seal the world championship, and he grabbed his chance with both hands.

Born in Frome, England, in 1980, Button lived with his father, a famed rallycross driver, after his parents divorced. Jenson idolized his dad and wanted to race from a young age. When he started karting, it was immediately clear that the apple hadn't fallen far from the tree. At eighteen, he moved into single-seaters, winning the Formula Ford championship on his first attempt. More success followed the next year in Formula 3, where he was the top rookie and classified third. After conducting a few tests in F1 machinery, he was granted his big break and an F1 contract with Williams for 2000, scoring points in just his second race.

At season's end, he was loaned to Renault for the next two years before moving to the BAR team in 2003. Young, good-looking, and quick-witted, Button was a PR dream. But his courting of tabloid headlines and a fun-loving lifestyle led to criticism from certain sections of the paddock that he was more interested in parties than applying himself to his racing, though all were aware of how fast he truly was, with an almost effortless driving style framed with purpose and grace. Despite a fast car through 2004 and 2005, wins eluded him. Then in

2006, in changeable conditions during a topsy-turvy race, he took his shot and won in Hungary.

After Honda took over the BAR team and produced poor cars, Button's career went downhill fast. When Honda withdrew from the sport at the end of 2008, it looked as though Button's time in Formula 1 was over with just one win to show for all his potent promise. Then the remains of the team were bought by Ross Brawn, their new car finally hit the track, and Button knew his chance had come.

The car was a rocket ship, and the Englishman took pole and the victory at the opening two races. Indeed, he won six of the opening seven races. The little team struggled to out-develop their rivals, who caught up to Brawn as the season progressed, but Button had done enough in the first half of the season, and against all odds, both he and Brawn were crowned the 2009 world champions.

Button moved to McLaren in 2010 and spent the next seven years at the team, outscoring his team-mate Sir Lewis Hamilton to finish second in 2011 and winning a further eight races before retiring at the end of 2016. He raced in Super GT in Japan, winning the championship, and made a one-off Formula 1 comeback at Monaco in 2017.

Today, Jenson Button lives in America with his wife and children, is a popular television pundit, and still continues to race, contesting races and championships as varied as the 24 Hours of Le Mans and NASCAR.

ROBERT KUBICA

The tale of Robert Kubica is a story of what might have been. The first Polish racer to compete in Formula 1, Kubica was the driver the great champions of the era all rated the highest. But an accident, from which he was lucky to escape with his life, changed everything.

Born in 1984, Kubica developed a love for driving at an early age, practicing in karts until he was allowed to enter competition at age ten, winning six championships in three years. He moved to Italy while still in his early teens, living in the factory of his karting team and sleeping on the floor. He simply lived for racing and became one of the most highly regarded and sought-after racers of his generation.

He was taken into Renault's young driver program as he began single-seater racing, finishing second in the Italian Formula Renault championship before winning the Renault World Series title in 2005. His success brought him to the attention of the BMW F1 team, who signed him as their reserve driver for 2006. When Jacques Villeneuve left the team midseason, Kubica was promoted to the full-time race seat, outqualifying his teammate on debut.

In 2007, Kubica developed into a consistent points scorer, but as his star ascended, he was involved in a horrific 300 kph, 75 G accident at the Canadian Grand Prix. Amazingly, he missed just one race after the accident, returning to qualify and finish fourth. He stayed with BMW for 2008, and while the season is most remembered for the championship fight between Ferrari's Felipe Massa and McLaren's Sir Lewis Hamilton, for much of the year Kubica was well in the title hunt. He won his first and only Grand Prix at the scene of his huge accident the year before, which brought him to the top of the standings. BMW, however, believed 2009 represented a better chance for them to fight, and as they focused on the next season, his car fell out of championship contention.

But 2009 was nowhere near as competitive a season for the team, and when BMW pulled out of the sport at the end of the year, Kubica was a free agent. In 2010, he returned to Renault, the team that had supported his early career, and scored three podiums. Then he signed a pre-contract to race for Ferrari in 2012. But his big chance never came. A racer through and through, Kubica loved competing wherever he could, and had taken to occasional rally outings. In early 2011, he entered the Rally Italia Sardegna and was involved in a huge crash, his car leaving the road and striking a metal barrier, which partially severed his right forearm. He kept his arm, but his mobility was limited and his racing career was, seemingly, over.

Incredibly, Kubica returned to race in the World Rally Championship and later to a full-time seat in Formula 1 with the Williams team. His racing exploits continued in sportscars, where he was crowned 2023 LMP2 champion. While never achieving the success his talent merited in F1, Kubica is viewed by the likes of Sir Lewis Hamilton and Fernando Alonso as one of the toughest rivals they ever faced. Had fate dealt him a different hand, one can only wonder what he might have achieved in that Ferrari seat in the 2010s.

THE 2000S

FELIPE MASSA

Felipe Massa was world champion for thirty seconds in 2008, crossing the line at his home race in São Paulo, Brazil, victorious and with enough points to take the crown. But half a minute later, with a change of positions on the last corner of the last lap, Sir Lewis Hamilton made up the additional point he needed to deny Massa the title. The plucky Brazilian was sidelined for much of 2009 after suffering a head injury in a freak accident, and he never again fought for a title.

RUBENS BARRICHELLO

Rarely has there been a more universally adored racer than Rubens Barrichello, the ever-cheerful Brazilian who combined raw speed with consistency and unflinching loyalty to his teams and his sport. He played the dutiful number two to Michael Schumacher through Ferrari's era of domination, helping them to numerous championships before aiding Brawn in their giant-killing 2009 season. He raced in Formula 1 for nineteen seasons before moving to IndyCar and, since 2012, Brazilian stock cars and taking multiple titles.

DAVID COULTHARD

David Coulthard's arrival in Formula 1 came in tragic circumstances, as he was drafted into the Williams team's race seat after the death of Ayrton Senna. But Coulthard was never just a stand-in; his talent was clear from his earliest years. He became a multiple race winner and eventually a stalwart of the McLaren team, forming a magnificent partnership with Mika Häkkinen. He shone throughout the 1990s and 2000s, but his best year came in 2001, when he ran home second behind Michael Schumacher. He saw out his F1 career at Red Bull, where he helped create the foundations on which their future success was built.

JUAN PABLO MONTOYA

An IndyCar champion and Indy 500 winner, Juan Pablo Montoya was the last driver to successfully transition from Indy to Formula 1. He was an old-school racer, aggressive and elbows out. With seemingly no fear, he took the fight to the established order from his very first F1 race, much to the surprise of the likes of Michael Schumacher, who'd never raced anyone quite like the Colombian. In any other era, he might have been world champion, but so dominant was Ferrari at the time that he never had the chance to battle for the ultimate crown. Although he only raced in Formula 1 for five and a half years, he is widely regarded as one of the best Formula 1 drivers of his generation.

TITANS OF THE 2000s

FERRARI

Ferrari ended the 1990s with the team's first Constructors' World Championship since the early 1980s, but the golden chalice remained the Drivers' Championship. And in 2000, twenty-one years after Jody Scheckter had last won a Drivers' Championship for Ferrari, Michael Schumacher began a run of five consecutive world titles with the Scuderia. At the time, Ferrari's six in a row and Schumacher's five was a record that few thought would ever be beaten. Schumacher was so dominant in 2002 that he won the title at the French Grand Prix... in June, with half the world championship still to be run! The team took 117 podiums and 57 wins in the 85 races from 2000 to the end of 2004, setting a new benchmark in Formula 1 history. Schumacher retired at the end of 2006, having lost out to Renault and Fernando Alonso in his last two seasons, but Ferrari rediscovered its form soon after, with Kimi Räikkönen joining from McLaren and winning the title in his first season with the team in 2007. Ferrari truly was the team to beat in the 2000s.

RENAULT

In 2000, Renault agreed to purchase the Benetton F1 team, and in 2002 the French manufacturer officially returned to F1 as a constructor. The team really started to make waves in 2003 when it brought on the Spanish youngster Fernando Alonso, who won his first Grand Prix that year. Renault very nearly came second in the 2004 world championship after a breakthrough season, but it was in 2005 and 2006 that they hit the headlines. With Alonso as their lead driver and Giancarlo Fisichella as his team-mate, Renault swept back-to-back titles, with Alonso taking the drivers' crown in both seasons. In a bid to win the Singapore Grand Prix in 2008, Renault forced their second driver, Nelson Piquet Jr, to crash on their orders, bringing out a safety car that helped Alonso claim victory. Renault was threatened with removal from the championship, and team boss Flavio Briatore was banned from playing a role in the sport for many years.

BRAWN GP

BAR (British American Racing) joined Formula 1 in 1999, fielding 1997 world champion Jacques Villeneuve. Established by Villeneuve's manager Craig Pollock, the team pulled in support from Honda, and by the mid-2000s it was a regular podium challenger, with Jenson Button eventually taking over as the team's number-one driver. At the end of 2005, Honda bought the team, and in 2006, it took its first win with Button in Hungary. But as results tailed off through 2007 and 2008, Honda shocked the sport and withdrew at season's end. Having invested heavily in the new regulation package for 2009, however, Honda sold the remnants of the squad to Ross Brawn, and Brawn GP proved the dominant team of the early part of the year due to using a double diffuser that exploited a loophole in the rules. As the larger teams out-developed Brawn, the team somehow held on to their championship leads, and in 2009, Jenson Button and Brawn GP were crowned world champions. At season's end Brawn sold the team to Mercedes, and the most incredible decade reached its conclusion for the team based in Brackley.

McLAREN

McLaren was a constant force in the 2000s, but it was unable to put it all together to win the Drivers' Championship until 2008. That period included six years where Adrian Newey remained as chief designer at the team, and his MP4/15-20 cars brought the squad numerous wins for Mika Häkkinen, David Coulthard, Kimi Räikkönen, and Juan Pablo Montoya. But against the might of Ferrari, McLaren just didn't have the edge that had marked them out in previous eras. Newey left to join the new Red Bull Racing team in 2006, and that season McLaren failed to win a single race. But things turned around in 2007 when new drivers Fernando Alonso and Sir Lewis Hamilton proved to be the class of the field in the MP4/23. But as the racers became rivals and took points off each other, Ferrari again pounced to win the drivers' and constructors' titles—and McLaren was excluded from the season for receiving a dossier of Ferrari design secrets. Hamilton and McLaren made amends the next year, taking the Drivers' Championship, but Ferrari again held on to the constructors' title. Incredibly, McLaren's last team title remains the one it took back in 1998, over a quarter of a century ago.

WILLIAMS

Williams began the 2000s with a new engine partner in BMW and a rookie driver in Jenson Button, but it fell to the team's established driver Ralf Schumacher to pull in the bulk of results. Button was dropped for IndyCar champion Juan Pablo Montoya for 2001, and the brilliant-but-fragile FW23 was worth more than the third place it took in the championship. Ferrari dominated in 2002, but Montoya's seven poles showed what might have been without Ferrari's race strength. In 2003, Williams came the closest it would to the title since its glory days of the 1990s—Montoya finished third, just eleven points behind Michael Schumacher. When BMW took over the Sauber team—and took its engine supply with them—Williams was forced to move to Cosworth and then Toyota power. The team failed to win another race for the rest of the decade.

BMW

BMW had long partnered Williams as engine provider and had achieved race wins and a run on the championship, but it struggled against the might of Ferrari in the early years of the decade. Things turned around when the manufacturer took a controlling interest in the Sauber team. Both 2007 and 2008 proved to be exceptional years for the squad, as their lead driver Robert Kubica won in Canada in 2008 just one year after a massive accident there. The team could have fought for the title in 2008 but chose to focus on a serious assault in 2009 instead. But when the new car didn't hit the marks under the new regulations, BMW thought better of it and quit the sport.

TOYOTA

Toyota entered Formula 1 with a big budget and big ambitions. Joining at the start of the 2002 season, their intentions were clear from the outset: to take on the established order and win. But despite an almost limitless budget and incredible facilities, they never got close. Just thirteen podiums in eight years was scant reward for the investment and effort put in by a team and manufacturer that had achieved so much in other forms of racing. When Toyota's parent company made a financial loss for the first time in its history in 2009, it had the perfect excuse to withdraw immediately from the sport. Today, Toyota focuses on rally and endurance racing, where it has proven to be substantially more competitive and has won multiple championships.

RACE OF THE DECADE

2005 JAPANESE GRAND PRIX

In the early 2000s, Formula 1 employed a qualifying format that often led to drivers starting races out of position. Regardless of the many versions it took, the one unifying factor was that it centered on drivers running on track alone for one single flying lap. No do-overs. No second chances. One-shot, single-lap qualifying. Whatever your time was over the line, that was all you got for the session.

In Japan in 2005, rain fell to varying degrees during single-lap qualifying on Saturday. This meant that drivers had all qualified in different conditions, and so the grid for Sunday's race was about as wildly shaken up as imaginable. Ralf Schumacher took pole for Toyota ahead of Jenson Button's BAR Honda and Giancarlo Fisichella's Renault. Michael Schumacher started fourteenth for Ferrari. Fernando Alonso was sixteenth in his Renault. The two McLarens of Kimi Räikkönen and Juan Pablo Montoya were seventeenth and eighteenth.

The race took place under cloudy skies, but the rain held off, and Formula 1 was treated to a magnificent race of recovery drives, as all those starting out of their expected positions fought to make their way back through the field. Fisichella was left in control of the race after Ralf Schumacher pitted early, but the battle behind had everyone captivated. Alonso made up nine positions on his first lap alone, and by lap nineteen he was in the wheel tracks of rival Michael Schumacher. Approaching the terrifyingly fast 130R left-hand corner, Alonso went to the outside and pulled off one of the most fearless overtaking maneuvers in the history of the sport.

It took Räikkönen a further ten laps, but he, too, put the move on Schumacher. Alonso, having now stopped for fuel, made his way back past the German on lap thirty-two. Renault by now was well aware that Räikkönen's pace was insatiable, and when race leader Fisichella took his last stop, the Finn was left in clean air at the head of the field. He pumped in the quick laps and eventually took his final stop on lap forty-five, emerging in second place to set off after Fisichella once again. With just a handful of laps remaining, Räikkönen was right with the Italian but could find no way past. As the final lap began, he lined up the Renault down the main straight and flew past at the first corner to the roar of the crowd, sealing a magnificent victory from seventeenth on the grid. Fisichella held on for second, with Alonso an excellent third from sixteenth.

One-lap qualifying was replaced at the end of the year, but the 2005 Japanese Grand Prix will forever be remembered as the day when a novel qualifying format provided the foundations of one of the most exhilarating races in history.

THE

20i

THE 2010S BEGAN AS a time of upheaval in Formula 1. The major manufacturers were spooked following the withdrawal of both Honda and Toyota, and they were facing major regulation changes designed to tighten the financial belts of the teams while simultaneously improving the show. The result was a decade in which two teams—one independent, one factory-based, and both relatively new to the game—dominated as two of the sport's great champion drivers racked up title after title.

In-race refueling was banned as soon as the decade began, and engine and gearbox allocations were shrunk to further limit costs. Innovations such as movable wings, reactive ride heights, and complex engine maps were banned, and a massive limit on testing was introduced to bring down expenditure. After teams started developing systems to stall the rear wing in order to give extra straight-line speed, rather than ban the innovation, the sport oversaw its evolution into the drag reduction system (DRS), which was made mandatory to help with overtaking.

By far the biggest change came in 2014 when Formula 1 entered its hybrid era. Out went the normally aspirated V8s, replaced by turbocharged, 1.6-liter V6 engines. These heavily complex power units pushed the developmental arc of the internal combustion engine, helping auto manufacturers achieve levels of efficiency never before seen on racetracks or on the road.

The new units didn't gain universal approval, however, in large part due to their low droning sound, which was a stark contrast to the shrieking, high-revving V8s, V10s, and V12s of the past.

With points now scored by the top-ten finishers, the early part of the decade was ruled by Red Bull Racing. The brilliant mind of designer Adrian Newey once again created championship-winning cars for an independent team, this time led by young German superstar Sebastian Vettel. Together, they took four double titles in a row. But once the turbo-hybrid era began, a familiar name leapt to the front. Mercedes hadn't raced in Formula 1 as a factory outfit since 1955, but in 2010, it returned, purchasing the Brawn GP outfit and setting up camp in the factory that had originally been built by BAR. Initially under the leadership of Ross Brawn, and then of Toto Wolff and Niki Lauda, the squad convinced Sir Lewis Hamilton to leave McLaren and join their mission for the world championship. They created the most effective team Formula 1 had ever known, smashing Ferrari's previous records to win eight Constructors' and seven Drivers' Championships in a row.

There was a seismic shift in the politics of Formula 1, as Max Mosley and Bernie Ecclestone's rule of the sport came to an end. Mosley's personal life had become the focus of tabloid headlines in the late 2000s, and former Ferrari team boss Jean Todt stepped into his place as president of the FIA. Ecclestone's financial control of Formula 1 had come under increasing regulatory scrutiny in the 2000s, and varying percentages of his companies and control of the sport had been sold and resold to banks, investment firms, and media companies into the 2010s. In 2016, however, Liberty Media bought the sport, and the new modern era of Formula 1 truly began with a comprehensive and cohesive push to make it the biggest and most dynamic sports entity in the world. Ecclestone, whose public statements increasingly fell out of step with the modern age and global reach of the sport he'd been instrumental in creating, became a peripheral figure.

There was tragedy to contend with, however. Twenty years after Formula 1's last fatality, the promising and hugely popular young French driver Jules Bianchi died as a result of an accident at the 2014 Japanese Grand Prix. As part of the Ferrari junior team, he'd long been expected to race for the Scuderia in the future, and his passing sent shockwaves through the sport. Formula 1 redoubled its safety efforts, developing two new concepts to better protect drivers in the cockpit. The aeroscreen, a roof-less canopy, eventually became mandatory in IndyCar. Formula 1 proceeded with its sister innovation, the halo, a wishbone-shaped protective bar wrapped around the cockpit that could take the weight of a London bus and disperse large objects away from the driver's head. The halo became mandatory in 2018.

Bianchi had been racing for Marussia, one of three new teams that joined Formula 1 in 2010. By 2017, none remained in the sport, as the financial and competitive mountain became simply too steep to climb. But into the void stepped Haas, an American NASCAR team with big ambitions. They scored points in just their second race and finished fifth in the Constructors' Championship in only their second season.

American interest in Formula 1 grew in the second half of the decade as the global appeal of the sport reached new heights. Under Liberty's new direction, Formula 1 became the fastest-growing sports league on Earth, embracing new media and promoting itself via linear and digital streams to new viewers. In 2019, Liberty's vision saw the release of *Formula 1: Drive to Survive*, a behind-the-scenes Netflix documentary series that followed Formula 1 around the world on an annual calendar, which now far exceeded twenty races, introducing the sport to a brand-new and ever-growing audience.

Formula 1 now raced from the Middle East to China, Russia to Singapore, Australia to Azerbaijan. From the traditions of a European-based championship, the old heartland of Formula 1 now accounted for less than half of the races on the calendar. F1 had become a bona fide phenomenon and was no longer a niche sport for the few. It had gone global.

SEBASTIAN VETTEL

《 4X CHAMPION 》

It was clear from the outset that Sebastian Vettel was destined for the Formula 1 World Championship. An intelligent, humble, and affable family man, he was the polar opposite in a race car, with a clinical and ruthless side that proved crucial to achieving the highest heights of the sport he loved.

Born in Heppenheim, Germany, in 1987, Vettel was driving karts by age three and competing by age eight. His talent impressed his hero Michael Schumacher, who became a mentor to his young compatriot. His pace also caught the attention of Red Bull, which brought him into their driver academy. He made his single-seater debut in German Formula BMW in 2003, and in 2004 he won eighteen of twenty races, finishing on the podium in the other two, to be crowned a dominant champion.

He took the standard progression to Formula 3 for two seasons before a stint in the 2007 Renault World Series, which coincided with a role at the BMW F1 team as their reserve driver. When Robert Kubica was ruled out of the US Grand Prix, Vettel was handed his F1 debut. He scored points, convincing Red Bull not to waste another second, and he saw out the remainder of the 2007 season with their junior team Toro Rosso.

The team was not a race-winning outfit and had never even scored a podium. But in 2008, in dreadfully wet conditions, Vettel took his Toro Rosso to the team's first ever pole and the win—becoming the youngest driver in history to do so. Red Bull had seen all they needed to and promoted him to their lead team for 2009. He won four Grands Prix and finished second in the championship.

From 2010, the combination of a confident and increasingly experienced Vettel, a car designed to his exact liking, and a team all pulling for him resulted in a period of domination. So perfectly attuned were driver and team that the Red Bull/Vettel combination drew comparisons with Schumacher and Ferrari's perfection of the 2000s. Together, over the next four seasons, they won thirty-four races and took every driver and team title over that period.

For Vettel, the chance to walk in the shoes of his great hero led him to make a shock move to Ferrari in 2015, where he would lead an ultimately fruitless attempt to recapture the world championship for the Scuderia. Despite Vettel challenging Sir Lewis Hamilton in 2017 and 2018, Mercedes was too strong, and all Vettel had to show for six years of hard work was eight race wins and two second-place championship finishes.

After becoming a father, Vettel finished the last two years of his racing career at Aston Martin. But with his cars rarely at a competitive level, his focus shifted away from the racetrack, and he used his platform to become a vocal advocate for a number of environmental and human-rights charities and causes. He retired at the end of the 2022 F1 season to focus on his family and the advocacy that had become so important to him.

THE 2010s

NICO
ROSBERG

《 1X CHAMPION 》

Nico Rosberg became only the second driver in Formula 1 history to emulate his father and also become world champion. In so doing, he achieved what so few ever have in beating Sir Lewis Hamilton over the course of a season in the same machinery. With two world champions set to be lined up against each other at Mercedes, the Formula 1 world held its breath for fireworks. But at the height of his powers, Rosberg sensationally announced his immediate retirement and never raced in Formula 1 again.

Born in Germany in 1985, Nico Rosberg was raised in Monaco but took the German nationality of his mother for his racing career. He was an intelligent and hardworking student, excelling at school and speaking multiple languages. He was offered a place at London's Imperial College to study aeronautical engineering, but to do so, he knew he would have to quit racing.

His decision to carry on competing was based on a junior career of some note, but not exactly one that indicated the raw potential of a future world champion. Sure, he won the Formula BMW title, but thereafter a few wins littered across a couple of Formula 3 seasons didn't exactly shout "megastar." During the inaugural year of the GP2 championship, however, people started to consider him a serious prospect, as he beat far more experienced and favored rivals to take the title. After that, he got promoted to Formula 1 with Williams. Like many champions, he managed to score points on debut in 2006.

When Mercedes re-entered the sport in 2010, it decided to do so with a big-name all-German lineup, convincing Michael Schumacher to come out of retirement and placing Rosberg as the up-and-coming German alongside him. Those early years at Mercedes worked wonders for Rosberg's reputation, as he didn't just match Schumacher but proved consistently faster. He took Mercedes' first F1 win since 1955 at the 2012 Chinese Grand Prix. In 2013, he was joined by his former karting team-mate Sir Lewis Hamilton, but what began as a friendly rivalry quickly descended into outright war as the pair became distrustful and resentful of each other.

Rosberg's style was always methodical and precise—he was a notoriously clean racer. But his personality could be awkward, and many found him to be grating and arrogant. In the end, those same personality traits proved to be key for developing the laser-focused selfishness that allowed him to fight for and win the world championship in 2016 in the final Grand Prix of an incredibly close season.

Rosberg realized that the sacrifices he'd made and the resolve it took to win the title had made him a different man, taking him away from the husband and father he wanted to be. A matter of days after winning the title, he announced his immediate retirement and walked away from Formula 1. Today, Rosberg runs an off-road team in Extreme E and dedicates much of his time to philanthropic work.

THE 2010S

DANIEL
RICCIARDO

Daniel Ricciardo's story is one of the most frustrating in modern-day Formula 1. Universally loved and respected as one of the most instinctive overtakers of his generation, his decline from a driver on the edge of greatness to having to start all over again has been as amazing as it was once unfathomable.

Ricciardo was born in Perth, Australia, in 1989. His early promise brought him to the attention of Red Bull, which signed him to their academy at the end of 2007. He won Formula BMW, Formula Renault, and British Formula 3 titles before moving to the Renault World Series, where he took an impressive second in the title race in his rookie year. He got his Formula 1 debut in 2011 with HRT, the slowest team in the sport, as Red Bull wanted to evaluate him as a potential racer for their teams. Ricciardo impressed enough to get a race seat at Toro Rosso for 2012, and he was brought into the top team to partner Sebastian Vettel in 2014.

After taking four titles in a row from 2010 to 2013, Vettel failed to win a single race in that 2014 season as Daniel Ricciardo swept to his first three Grand Prix victories. Vettel finished the season fifth. Ricciardo was third. Red Bull had seemingly found their new champion, and when Vettel announced he was leaving for Ferrari, Ricciardo stepped up to be team leader. But Ricciardo's arrival at the helm of Red Bull coincided with their decline. As race retirements mounted, Ricciardo's frustrations set in. When Red Bull signed Max Verstappen to be Ricciardo's new partner for 2016 and the team began to mold itself around its new future star, the Australian believed the writing was on the wall. Ricciardo departed for Renault and

after two seasons with the French team went on to race for McLaren.

The ever-smiling Australian is one of the most-liked members of the paddock. Yet as the years rolled by and the results failed to come, Ricciardo's trademark smile slipped. He struggled to understand why he was failing to get to grips with his cars, and by the end of 2022, he'd quite simply had enough. His confidence and mental health had taken such a hit that he needed time away from the sport to figure out it if he even wanted to race anymore.

In 2023, Red Bull offered Ricciardo a lifeline, and he returned as a reserve driver to the team he should perhaps have never left. But when Red Bull's junior team's lineup failed to meet expectations, the Australian received an unexpected call-up in the middle of the season to return to racing at Scuderia AlphaTauri. But after just two races, a crash in practice for the Dutch Grand Prix broke a bone in his hand and forced him back onto the sidelines. Despite his rocky road, he was announced as a full-time racer for AlphaTauri for 2024, back to where he'd spent his first full-time season in F1 twelve years before.

It is the grandest of ironies that Ricciardo and Verstappen formed the most potent lineup Red Bull had seen since its championship-winning days, and yet he left the team just as it was about to regain its competitive edge. Had he stayed rather than left in search of number-one status, there are very few within the sport who don't think that Daniel Ricciardo would have won at least one world championship by now.

THE 2010S

BEST OF THE REST: 2010s

VALTTERI BOTTAS

Finland's Valtteri Bottas had a junior career of dreams, dominating karting and the single-seater ladder to arrive in Formula 1 as the man to watch. As Bottas scored podiums and fastest laps for the declining Williams team, Mercedes turned to him to fill Nico Rosberg's shoes after Rosberg announced his retirement. Ruthlessly fast over one lap, his race pace could sometimes prove frustrating, but he was a quick and determined team-mate to Sir Lewis Hamilton, who liked and deeply respected him.

MARK WEBBER

Mark Webber became a fan favorite in just his first race, scoring points at home in Australia for the unfavored Minardi team. In a career that took him to Jaguar, Williams, and finally Red Bull, Webber became a multiple race winner and key part of the team that would dominate the opening years of the 2010s. Although he became frustrated with his perceived number-two billing at Red Bull, he came close to the championship, finishing third on three occasions. After Formula 1, Webber moved into sportscars, winning the World Endurance Championship and finishing second at Le Mans.

ROMAIN GROSJEAN

Frenchman Romain Grosjean was one of the highest-regarded drivers in junior formulas, winning the title in every category he entered, but a combination of bad luck and bad judgment meant that his Formula 1 career never lived up to expectations. He had two stints in the sport, racing for Lotus and Haas, and while podiums were as good as things got, on his day he was one of the fastest racers in the sport. He survived a terrifying fireball accident at the end of his final season in Formula 1, adopting the nickname "the Phoenix" for his new career in IndyCar, where he races today.

SUSIE WOLFF

Susie Stoddart was an impressive karter, winning in her native Scotland before embarking on European and international championships. She rose to prominence competing in Formula Renault and Formula 3 before shifting away from single-seaters to compete in German touring cars, where she met and married Austrian racer Toto Wolff. In 2012, she became a development driver for the Williams F1 team, and in 2014 and 2015, she took part in Grand Prix weekend practice sessions for the team, proving to be competitive in an otherwise all-male field. With chances to race slim, she moved into team management in Formula E before shifting focus to run the F1 Academy, which is training a new generation of female racers.

MERCEDES

Mercedes returned to Formula 1 in 2010 after a fifty-five-year gap from their last entry as a manufacturer, purchasing the Brawn GP team that had won the world championships in 2009. Convincing legend Michael Schumacher to come out of retirement and partnering him with young compatriot Nico Rosberg was brilliant marketing for the German auto manufacturer, but Schumacher was a shadow of his former self, and it was Rosberg who routinely had the upper hand. The team, initially under the leadership of Ross Brawn but later run by Toto Wolff and Niki Lauda, convinced Sir Lewis Hamilton to join from McLaren, and it was at this point that the team's fortunes changed. The combination of the dawn of the hybrid era in Formula 1 and the incredible technical leadership of James Allison and Aldo Costa meant that Mercedes dominated the decade, winning eight Constructors' World Championships in a row. From the start of the hybrid era, Mercedes took every drivers' title, too: Hamilton in 2014 and 2015, Rosberg in 2016, and Hamilton again in 2017, 2018, and 2019. It wasn't all smooth sailing, though, as former childhood friends Rosberg and Hamilton fell out, leading to Rosberg's immediate retirement on winning the crown. But with Toto Wolff at the helm, Mercedes became one of the most efficient and dominant outfits the sport had ever seen.

RED BULL RACING

Former racer Christian Horner had been a successful team owner in F1's feeder championships, and in his years in the junior leagues he had forged a close working relationship with the Red Bull academy of drivers. So when the drinks company decided to launch an F1 team, he was the natural choice to lead it. Aided by former F1 driver Helmut Marko as advisor and Adrian Newey as chief designer, Red Bull Racing became the dominant team of the early 2010s. The team began as an outfit notorious more for their post-race parties than their on-track results, but when the stars aligned and Red Bull elevated Sebastian Vettel to lead driver, things got serious. Red Bull became one of the slickest outfits in the sport, known for producing aerodynamically masterful cars, tremendously fast pitstops, and clever strategies. They maintained their fun side, but never again at the expense of on-track success. Winning four titles on the bounce to kick-start the decade, they fell back once the hybrid era began and customer engine supply became a headache. Red Bull eventually lost Vettel to Ferrari, but in Daniel Ricciardo and eventually young sensation Max Verstappen, the team found the drivers to continue winning, which established the basis for their push back to championship success in the 2020s.

FERRARI

Ferrari went through a period of huge change in the 2010s, moving through a number of team bosses and drivers. Yet championship success somehow eluded the team throughout the decade despite some real chances and near misses. Ferrari's best shots came under team boss Stefano Domenicali, and with Fernando Alonso as the lead driver, the team battled with Red Bull in the final years of normally aspirated engines. Alonso missed out on the championship by mere points in both 2010 and 2012, and when Ferrari signed Sebastian Vettel to replace him, they formed the most consistent challenger to Mercedes in the latter half of the decade. Yet that second half of the 2010s took place under the controversial leadership of Maurizio Arrivabene, who instilled in the team a bunker mentality of fear-based rule. Things never quite gelled for Vettel, and despite multiple wins, his dream of emulating his childhood hero Michael Schumacher in returning Ferrari to their glory days never transpired. In 2019, Mattia Binotto, who like Domenicali had risen through the ranks at the team, took over at the helm, signing young drivers to begin a new era at Ferrari.

McLAREN

The 2010s began with McLaren as the most regular challenger to Red Bull's might, but a number of key decisions swept it from the top of the pecking order to one of the most difficult periods in the team's history. The combination of losing Sir Lewis Hamilton to Mercedes and then taking a chance on a partnership with Honda proved catastrophic. Despite a rich turbo history, Honda returned to Formula 1 on the back foot, much of which was due to the restrictions placed on their engine design by McLaren themselves. Fernando Alonso returned to the team alongside 2009 world champion Jenson Button, but as politics at the team played out and team boss Ron Dennis was ousted from the powerhouse he'd created, it all came unstuck. McLaren came ninth out of ten teams in 2015 and 2017, but their fortunes took an upturn when marketeer and racer Zak Brown was appointed CEO. The team switched to Renault engines, and by the end of the decade they had repositioned themselves behind only the top three teams.

FORCE INDIA

The Jordan team was sold in the mid-2000s and thereafter went through many guises until it was finally purchased by Indian billionaire Vijay Mallya, creating the Force India F1 team. Still operating from Eddie Jordan's factory at Silverstone, the team became known as a giant killer in the sport because, despite never having the budget of the major players, they consistently created effective cars and pulled off strategic master classes to steal big points hauls and podiums. By the end of the decade, however, Mallya faced political and financial problems, and the team was put into administration. Eventually, Canadian billionaire Lawrence Stroll purchased and saved the team, which continued under the name of Racing Point. Rebranded, the team won its first race with Sergio Perez at the penultimate Grand Prix of the 2010s.

WILLIAMS

WILLIAMS F1 TEAM

Williams had a roller-coaster decade in the 2010s, bouncing from back of the pack to podiums and back to the bottom. The team ran three different engines throughout the period, moving from Cosworth power to Renault and finally Mercedes. Williams took a shock win, currently their last, at the 2012 Spanish Grand Prix, when seemingly out of nowhere Pastor Maldonado took both pole and victory. The beginning of the team's alliance with Mercedes signaled its last true period of effectiveness—it scored consistently in 2014 and 2015, and slightly less so in 2016 and 2017. Those first two years saw the team fighting for poles and podiums. But the team took a number of missteps, with cars delayed and often poorly designed. By the end of the decade, Williams was a shadow of the team that had been a championship winner in the 1980s and 1990s and found itself routinely at the back of the pack.

RACE OF THE DECADE

2011 CANADIAN GRAND PRIX

At over four hours in length, the 2011 Canadian Grand Prix was the longest race in Formula 1 history. Rain, safety cars, multiple pitstops, and some incredible overtaking also made it one of the most exciting. But it was the last lap move for the win, pulled off by a driver who at one point had been classified in last position, that cemented this as the race of the decade—and for many, the best race Formula 1 had ever seen. It was a perfect exemplification of never giving up because, in this sport, anything can happen.

In the midst of an era of Red Bull domination, it was no surprise that reigning world champion Sebastian Vettel took pole position from the two Ferraris of Fernando Alonso and Felipe Massa. The German controlled the entire Grand Prix from the front. Rainstorms hit the circuit early on race day, and continuing storms wreaked havoc with strategy and the running of the race itself, which began behind the safety car and saw its intervention at numerous points throughout the afternoon.

Starting in seventh, McLaren's Jenson Button found himself battling his own team-mate Sir Lewis Hamilton in the early laps, and when the pair made contact, Hamilton was forced into retirement. Button yo-yoed up and down the order, fighting into the points, then falling down again as pitstops for differing levels of wet-weather tires, punctures, drive-through penalties, and the replacement of a front wing saw him, at one point, in last place.

The race was even suspended as the rain fell so heavily that the cars couldn't stay on track, even using full wet tires. After a two-hour delay, the race got back under way again, and as Massa fought with Michael Schumacher and Sauber's Kamui Kobayashi for second, Alonso spun out of the race. Some drivers nevertheless decided to switch to slick tires, and as the track slightly dried, it became clear that they were the correct choice of race rubber.

Button was one of the drivers who made the early change to slicks, and by now he was finding grip everywhere, scything through the field. Hunting down race leader Vettel, Button was less than a second behind as the final lap began, and as he applied pressure, the Red Bull driver made a mistake. Button swept through to take the lead and an incredible race win ahead of the Red Bull duo.

It was the most astonishing afternoon of risk and reward, in which a driver who had seen almost every negative variable thrown at him still managed to pick his way through the field to win. It was the 2009 champion's day of days, by any metric his finest win, and to many observers one of the greatest races in what had then been six decades of Formula 1 Grands Prix.

THE 20

THE 2020S BEGAN WITH the world caught in the midst of a global pandemic. The international spread of Covid-19 shut down the freedom of movement and travel that everyone had taken for granted, with governments around the world mandating lockdowns and the cancellation of large events. The swiftness with which the restrictions took hold surprised everyone, and Formula 1 was no exception. During pre-season testing and car launches in 2020, the virus was a key topic of conversation, but nobody could have foretold how its spread would accelerate. The sport set itself up in Australia for the opening round of the season, but as quickly as the paddock was assembled, it was shut down, as cases of the virus were discovered within the traveling staff.

Formula 1 closed its gates and returned home, and for months, many wondered what would happen next. With no racing, teams turned their engineering expertise to helping their national health sectors, while in the background, Formula 1 and the FIA plotted a method by which racing could continue. In a matter of months, a new calendar was created. Based largely in Europe, it featured double-header races in Austria and Great Britain, and new host tracks for stand-alone events at Mugello in Italy, Portimão in Portugal, and a return to Imola, Turkey, and the Nürburgring in Germany.

In July 2020, a seventeen-race season began, with the entire paddock kept in strict team-by-team bubbles, with no interaction between these limited groups allowed. Masks were compulsory, media duties were carried out at a minimum six-foot distance, and every member of the paddock underwent Covid-19 tests every seventy-two hours at minimum. Sergio Pérez, Lance Stroll, and Sir Lewis Hamilton missed races after contracting the virus. But the championship and the sport continued, against all odds, becoming the first international sporting series to restart after the global lockdown. It was a triumph of organization and determination, and it became the blueprint for how other sports would continue throughout the pandemic.

A major regulation change had been planned for 2021, but given the nature of the 2020 season and the immense pull on resources, the new car designation was delayed for twelve months, ready to launch in 2022. The 2021 season therefore featured cars that were carryovers from 2020, and the season delivered a championship fight for the ages. With the calendar almost back to normal at twenty-two races, Sir Lewis Hamilton gunned for his eighth world championship with Mercedes against Max Verstappen, who was aiming for his first with Red Bull.

The title went to the wire. All season long, questions had been levied over the consistency of decisions made by Race Control over racing etiquette, with the championship rivals making contact on numerous occasions. The pressure started to weigh heavily on drivers, team bosses, and increasingly on the race director, who was being pulled deeper into the rolling narrative of the season. His decision to call a safety car in the final laps of the final race of the season will be debated for years to come, but it resulted in a thrilling last-lap showdown for the title.

Hamilton led on old tires. Verstappen sat second on fresh tires. The Dutchman made the move, won the race, and took the title. Mercedes and Hamilton were distraught. Red Bull and Verstappen were delirious. The sport's fans were either elated or confused, although the two reactions were by no means mutually exclusive.

A change in the FIA presidency over the winter saw the race director removed and replaced, and 2022 began with a new set of rules and a new generation of car. Out went the complex aerodynamics of the past, replaced by sleeker and simpler bodies designed to limit disrupted airflow and allow cars to follow each other more closely. Ground effect, which had been banned since the early 1980s, made a return as the major means by which cars would find their grip, being sucked toward the track rather than pushed down. Tires grew in diameter, from thirteen to eighteen inches. It was the single largest regulation change in F1 history, demanding teams to rip up their previous designs and start from scratch.

These huge changes came with a financial restriction placed on all teams to curb spending. Everyone faced the exact same limitations. The years of the big teams outspending the small teams were at an end. And development time was now only permitted on a sliding scale. The higher up the championship a team found themselves, the less time they would have to improve their cars in their wind tunnels and via computer simulations. All of this was designed to bring the field closer together, improve competitiveness, and create more exciting racing. And this was

all at a time when—thanks to Formula 1's ability to carry on throughout the dark days of the pandemic, as well as its desire to engage with a new audience discovering F1 and binging the now globally popular *Drive to Survive*—the sport's fan base was at an all-time high.

The 2020s have seen new young drivers making their mark in the sport, led by Max Verstappen, who emerged with Red Bull Racing as the combination to beat. Charles Leclerc, Carlos Sainz, George Russell, Esteban Ocon, and Pierre Gasly became race winners, signaling a changing of the guard and the beginning of a new generation of racing superstars. And yet the old masters have remained a constant thorn in their side, with Sir Lewis Hamilton and Fernando Alonso as sparkling on their day as they have ever been. But few have been able to hold a candle to Red Bull Racing and Max Verstappen, with the Dutchman taking three world championships in succession from 2021 to 2023, and with both driver and team setting a new record for consecutive wins along the way (though the perfect season remains unfulfilled).

As the sport looks to the future, it has planned new regulations for 2026. New auto manufacturers and some familiar names have vowed to return as the sport's footprint grows larger and Formula 1 embarks on its longest-ever seasons. Formula 1 has now become a global megasport, with movies once again being made about it and celebrities wanting to be seen at the world's most exhilarating racing spectacle. Formula 1 is headline news. A box office smash. The future has never looked brighter.

MAX VERSTAPPEN

A karting prodigy who rose to become the youngest Grand Prix winner in history and the target man of the 2020s, Max Verstappen is a phenomenon who has changed the face of Formula 1. For a multiple champion still developing and honing his craft, the only question that remains is just how many titles he will amass and how many records he will break over the course of his career.

The son of former F1 racer Jos Verstappen and karting star Sophie Kumpen, Verstappen had racing embedded in his genes. He grew up surrounded by motorsport, attending Grands Prix with his father as a child, and began racing himself almost as soon as he could walk. His natural ability became the stuff of legend, and combined with an aggressive and uncompromising style, Verstappen's reputation as a fierce competitor and racing prodigy took on a life of its own.

He dominated karts, firing through European and world championships to become the youngest driver on record to take most of the major titles. His first taste of open wheel competition came in 2014 at the age of sixteen when he contested the one-off Florida Winter Series in F4 machinery before his first and only season in F3 that same year. His raw ability saw him courted by Mercedes and Ferrari, but it was Red Bull that won his signature, and by the end of the year he was taking part in F1 practice sessions for the squad's junior team.

In March 2015, he made his F1 race debut for Toro Rosso at just seventeen years old, which is the youngest debut in F1 history. He impressed and was promoted early in his second season to Red Bull's top F1 team. He won his first race for that team, becoming the youngest race winner in history at the age of 18 years and 228 days. Yet for all his raw pace, he courted controversy. His aggression on the track and seemingly late defensive moves caught the ire of fellow drivers and the governing body, which created new rules to try to curb his distinct style. His youthful excess could boil over, and his focus was seemingly always on the moment rather than the bigger picture. But in an era when the long game and racing conservatively had become the norm, his focus on taking every opportunity brought him a legion of fans.

In 2021, he won his first world title, and in the process denied his season-long rival Sir Lewis Hamilton a record eighth crown. In 2022, he defeated Charles Leclerc and a rejuvenated Ferrari to take his second title. And in 2023, armed with more maturity, the ability to conserve tires, and an awareness that brought him closer to perfection, he crushed the opposition to take his third world championship, along the way setting a new record for consecutive Grand Prix victories.

Max Verstappen is the man everyone wants and needs to beat in the current era of Formula 1. Together with Red Bull Racing, he has created a new era of domination and already sits third on the list of most wins in F1 history.

THE CURRENT CROP

CHARLES LECLERC

A multiple Grand Prix winner, Charles Leclerc is renowned as one of the fastest modern F1 drivers over a single lap, his qualifying pace almost unrivaled in the sport. Hailing from Monaco, Leclerc fought for the title in 2022, yet a number of small personal and team errors amassed and saw him slip out of contention. He is so highly regarded that Ferrari rewarded him with the longest driver contract in the team's history, and a recent extension of that deal will see him race at the Scuderia for many years to come.

CARLOS SAINZ

Arriving in Formula 1 as a Red Bull junior driver and team-mate to Max Verstappen, Spain's Carlos Sainz has become one of the most-respected drivers in the current field, excelling with Red Bull's Toro Rosso team before leaving to embark on a career that has seen him race for Renault, McLaren, and Ferrari. His ability to read races and call strategy from the cockpit is deeply impressive, and his pace, commitment, and race-winning acumen have made him a keen favorite.

SERGIO PÉREZ

For years Mexico's Sergio Pérez stood one step away from finding himself behind the wheel of a car worthy of his talents. It was his time spent at the Force India team that honed a giant-killing pedigree, his first win coming in Bahrain in 2021 in a race that had at one point seen him classified in last place. When Red Bull realized that none of their junior drivers could handle the pace of Verstappen as a team-mate, they signed Pérez. With a championship-winning car at his disposal, he is a constant threat for poles and wins.

GEORGE RUSSELL

A junior series megastar, Britain's George Russell began his F1 career at a Williams team that routinely found itself at the back of the field. Such was his pace, however, that he was able to qualify the car far higher than it had a right to be. Eventually, his incredible performances were rewarded with a seat at one of the best teams in the sport, and he was called up to partner his childhood hero Sir Lewis Hamilton at Mercedes from 2022, where he will lead the team into its next generation.

PIERRE GASLY

France's Pierre Gasly was at one time a member of the Red Bull driver academy. Their backing aided him through his junior career and elevated him to Formula 1 and, quickly, to the lead team alongside Max Verstappen. But with results in short supply, Red Bull dropped him down to their junior team once again. For many drivers, such a demotion might have destroyed their confidence, but Gasly used it as motivation, and in 2020 at Monza, he took the team's second-ever win. Still rated as one of the best in the game, he races today for Alpine in an all-French driver lineup.

ESTEBAN OCON

Unlike many of his rivals, Frenchman Esteban Ocon did not come from a wealthy background. His parents sold their house and lived in a trailer to help fund his karting career, and their faith in their son embedded in him a fire to succeed. After years of impressive performances in smaller F1 teams, he received a call-up to race for French squad Alpine, and in 2021, he rewarded that team with his first Grand Prix victory at Hungary. He is a doggedly determined member of the new F1 generation.

LANDO NORRIS

Like George Russell, Lando Norris won pretty much everything in junior formulas on his way to Formula 1, becoming a keen favorite of the McLaren F1 team. Team boss Zak Brown brought him into the McLaren academy, and Norris has spent his entire F1 career with McLaren, taking numerous podiums along the way. Despite reportedly receiving offers to race for teams with a more recent championship-winning pedigree, he has stayed loyal to the team that has backed him for so many years.

ALEX ALBON

So good was Thailand's Alex Albon in karting that many of his modern day F1 rivals grew up with posters of him on their wall. Taken in by the Red Bull program in his youth, he was subsequently dropped and then picked up again as his results dipped and then excelled in junior categories. After racing for AlphaTauri and Red Bull, he now leads Williams on their quest back to the front in Formula 1.

OSCAR PIASTRI

Australia's Oscar Piastri ripped through the feeder series ladder, winning the F3 and F2 crowns to establish himself as the coming man in Formula 1. Employed as a reserve driver at Alpine, the team expected him to graduate to F1 with them when Fernando Alonso switched teams to Aston Martin. Unknown to Alpine, however, Piastri had already concluded a deal to race for McLaren. So highly regarded was he that a bitter legal fight ensued, which McLaren won, and he duly made his debut for the British team in 2023, impressing from the start and immediately showing why there had been such a fight for his services as he roared to a Sprint Race win in Qatar.

KEVIN MAGNUSSEN

Denmark's Kevin Magnussen had a glittering junior career and took a podium on his F1 debut in 2014 for McLaren, the team with which his father Jan had a relationship during his own brief F1 career. Since that first year, Magnussen has never had a car capable of displaying his true merits. After taking a year out to focus on sportscars, he made a comeback in 2021 with Haas, where a new maturity and focus has seen him become one of the most dependable hands in the game.

NICO HÜLKENBERG

The man with the least enviable record in Formula 1, Nico Hülkenberg is the driver with the most F1 starts to have never stood on a podium. Such a statistic seemed unfathomable when the German ace made his debut in 2010, since he had demolished the opposition in his junior racing days. Still racing and still hungry, he has now amassed over two hundred Grand Prix starts, but that podium remains, at the time of writing, elusive.

LANCE STROLL

Son of Canadian billionaire Lawrence Stroll, owner of the Aston Martin F1 Team, Lance Stroll is often written off as a rich kid who bought his way into the sport and benefits from the safety net of a race seat on a team owned by his father. But that simple explanation ignores his junior results and overlooks his ability to get the job done in Formula 1. He has taken pole positions and finished on the podium in cars few thought were capable of doing so. On his day, he has shown the pace to match the very best.

YUKI TSUNODA

Backed by Honda and recently Red Bull, Japan's Yuki Tsunoda arrived in Formula 1 to a whirlwind of praise. The diminutive racer is one of the punchiest of the bunch, often taking below-par equipment to incredible heights. While he has a reputation in the car for fiery outbursts, outside the cockpit he is mild-natured and loved by his teams. Tsunoda remains a consistently impressive racer who defies the odds.

ZHOU GUANYU

China's first-ever Grand Prix driver, Zhou Guanyu made his Formula 1 debut in 2022 lining up alongside the highly experienced race winner Valtteri Bottas at Alfa Romeo. Despite low expectations due to an unspectacular junior career, he more than made his mark and was swiftly up to speed, often outscoring his vastly more experienced team-mate.

LOGAN SARGEANT

The first full-time American F1 driver since 2007, Logan Sargeant graduated to Formula 1 after winning races in Formula 4, Formula 3, and Formula 2. While never taking the title in any of the junior categories, his consistency and work ethic impressed Williams enough to add him to their development roster in his formative years. In 2023, Williams took a chance on him as a race driver in the pinnacle of the sport and will give him a second year in F1 in 2024.

TODAY'S TEAMS

RED BULL RACING

Having found themselves on the back foot since the start of the turbo-hybrid era, in the 2020s Red Bull switched from Renault to Honda power units and immediately started to reap the rewards, as Honda moved on from their tumultuous experience with McLaren in the 2010s to become a dependable and incredibly competitive engine provider. The partnership saw Red Bull go from race winners to championship contenders, and in 2021, Max Verstappen took the team's first title since Sebastian Vettel's in 2013. With the dawn of the new car regulations in 2022, Red Bull's design genius Adrian Newey got everything right to create an almost perfect car, and Red Bull and Verstappen took drivers' and constructors' crowns in the first year of the new-look Formula 1. That didn't come without controversy, however, as an overspend on the budget cap saw Red Bull punished with an additional restriction in development time for 2023. Despite this, the team was able to deliver an even better car and demolished the opposition in a truly dominant season.

MERCEDES

Mercedes was the team to beat for the majority of the 2010s, but the switch-up in car design in 2022 caught out the best in the business. With a blank sheet of paper, Mercedes opted to go revolutionary with their design, creating a car that had almost no sidepods. But the unique aerodynamic concept, coupled with a flawed suspension design, left Mercedes trailing behind both Red Bull and Ferrari in 2022. The squad stuck to their guns for 2023, but after just one race abandoned the concept and made massive changes, moving toward a more traditional design in an attempt to catch Red Bull.

FERRARI

The new 2022 regulations gave Ferrari a chance to regain their place at the forefront of the sport, and that year they delivered easily their most competitive car of the turbo-hybrid era. Yet their failure to adequately develop the car, combined with basic strategy mistakes, left team principal Mattia Binotto, a Ferrari man of more than twenty years, in the firing line. He was replaced by Frédéric Vasseur, who had ruled junior category racing for twenty years with his own team running drivers like Sir Lewis Hamilton and Nico Rosberg in their developmental years. Vasseur and his newly emboldened Ferrari operation broke Red Bull's monopoly on the 2023 season, becoming the first (and only team) to beat Red Bull to a race win that season.

McLAREN

McLaren had hoped the new regulations would give them a chance to regain the form that made them one of the sport's most successful teams in the seventies, eighties, and nineties. Missteps in design direction, however, set their aspirations back considerably, and the team, which had fought for top-three honors at the turn of the decade, found themselves struggling to score points. Despite a few podiums and a win against the odds at Monza in 2021, McLaren made key changes to both the driver lineup and technical organization as it attempted to return to the front against an increasingly close and competitive 2020s field, impressing everyone with their rate of development in removing themselves from their struggles to once again find themselves fighting at the front.

ASTON MARTIN

ASTON MARTIN
FORMULA ONE™ TEAM

When Force India was put into administration, Canadian billionaire Lawrence Stroll bought the team, eventually rebranding it as Aston Martin after the British car company he owned. He injected money and positivity into the team, building a state-of-the-art facility and taking the team to the top of budget-cap spending. A recruitment drive brought some of the best design and technical minds in the sport to the squad, along with two-time champion Fernando Alonso, as Aston Martin set itself on a quest to become world champion by the middle of the decade.

ALPINE

ALPINE
F1˙ TEAM

The team formerly known as Toleman, Benetton, Renault, Lotus, and Renault (again) went through yet another transformation at the start of the decade to be rebranded as Alpine, one of the Renault car company's sportier brands. Under the restrictions of the budget cap, Alpine has consistently impressed with their intelligent use of funds to constantly improve their cars. It has proven to be a regular points scorer, has often been in contention for podiums, and has taken the occasional win.

SAUBER

Switzerland's Peter Sauber had run a Formula 1 team since the 1990s, at one time partnering with BMW as a race-winning outfit. At the turn of the 2010s, a naming deal with Italian brand Alfa Romeo saw the Swiss team take on a new identity, the famous name that had dominated the early years of Grand Prix racing. In 2024, Alfa Romeo was replaced as titular naming partner by Stake, by which name the team will be known for an interim period until Audi takes over the squad in 2026.

RB

Red Bull has always had two teams in Formula 1: the lead squad holding title aspirations, and a sister team established to train its junior drivers. Originally named Toro Rosso (Italian for "Red Bull"), the squad changed its name in the 2020s to that of Red Bull's clothing brand, AlphaTauri. Still seen as a junior team, it has always taken its chances when they arose, with Pierre Gasly famously winning the 2020 Italian Grand Prix. The team changed its name again in 2024, becoming known as RB, and despite setting the goal of being taken seriously in its own right, it controversially tightened its relationship with Red Bull.

WILLIAMS

Despite a tumultuous decade in the 2010s, Williams remains the second-most-successful team in the sport's history. Following the death of the team's founder Sir Frank Williams in 2021, the squad was sold to an American investment company, with the promise of a much-needed financial injection. In 2023, Williams employed James Vowles as team principal, a man who had been at the heart of the dominant Mercedes championship-winning team as their motorsport strategy director. He set about rebuilding the squad and after an impressive 2023 is working to return it to the front of the field.

HAAS

American businessman Gene Haas had run a NASCAR team for many years when he decided to enter Formula 1 in the mid-2010s. Using his business acumen, he determined to buy as many car parts as he could from Ferrari, manufacturing only what was absolutely necessary to be considered a "constructor" himself. Such a cost-saving method of F1 entry paid dividends in the early years, and points-scoring results came quickly. But as the rate of development in the sport became clear to him and his team, they slipped back. Other American teams have tried their hand at Formula 1, but none has contested as many races as Haas.

THE FUTURE

FORMULA 1 HAS NEVER STOOD still. From its earliest days, it has always looked to the future as the brilliant minds in the sport have consistently pushed the boundaries of mechanical and engineering know-how to develop machines at the cutting edge of technology. In the past such revolutions occurred solely for the benefit of competition, but today there is an additional and, many would argue, more important consideration.

As Formula 1 looks to its future, the sport has recognized the wider role it can play in society and is strategizing how the great fortunes spent by its teams—which employ some of the world's most incredible engineering minds—can be put to global use. In the heat of competition, evolution and technical revolution take place at accelerated speeds. Just as electronic driver aids in the 1980s and 1990s made their way from Formula 1 to road-going cars, FIA F1 crash tests were developed to create the Global NCAP (New Car Assessment Programme) by which all road cars are today now judged for vehicle safety, and the advent of hybrid power in Formula 1 advanced the efficiency of the internal combustion engine in the 2010s, so F1 can be a force for good today and into the future.

The sport is committed to pursuing a path toward sustainability and carbon neutrality, both for its own operations and that of its teams. New engine regulations are being plotted for the future, with multiple global brands keen to utilize the sport as a testing bed for new technologies. The hope is that in every area the sport is engaged, it can further the development of future tech with a global consciousness.

Formula 1 is also making great strides to ensure the paddock gates are open to all, with inclusion and equity at the heart of its future plans, and a new path through junior championships has been established to facilitate the next generation of female talent rising to the top of the sport to compete for the Formula 1 World Championship.

INCLUSION IN FORMULA 1

Despite Formula 1's global appeal, it has been seen for much of its existence as an elitist pursuit, most usually embarked upon by upper- and middle-class white European men. In the early 2020s, at a time of great social change, Formula 1 made a conscious effort—led by Sir Lewis Hamilton and F1's new owners, Liberty Media—to push for better representation and inclusion in all job roles within the sport.

Formula 1's first mission was to seek greater teaching of science, technology, engineering, and mathematics (STEM) at schools and to push for greater access to these subjects by historically marginalized and underrepresented groups, in order to open up career opportunities in motorsport engineering. In 2021, Formula 1 announced its first Engineering Degree scholarships at a variety of universities, all aimed at giving ethnic minorities, women, and those from lower socio-economic backgrounds the opportunity to follow their passions and work in motor racing.

Sir Lewis Hamilton established the Hamilton Commission in 2019, and its first report determined that only 1 percent of all employees within Formula 1 teams were Black. Societal hurdles were named as the biggest reason for such a low number. Hamilton subsequently established the Mission 44 charitable foundation, which is aimed at aiding education, employment, and empowerment. The charity seeks to build a more inclusive education system, creating clear pathways into STEM via early career opportunities and mentorship, and the creation of key links between social action opportunities, schools, and nonprofit organizations.

In 2023, Hamilton's team, Mercedes, confirmed that, along with their world champion driver, it had created the Ignite Partnership, a scholarship that offers funding to support Black individuals to study within the motorsport world at the UK's Royal Academy of Engineering. In addition, Mercedes launched its own Accelerate 25 program, which will see at least 25 percent of all new hires at the team come from underrepresented groups by 2025.

Female participation in the sport is at an all-time high, with women occupying prominent positions at all levels of Formula 1, from the factory floor to the pit wall and from the garage to the boardroom. Formula 1 today prides itself on being a place where talent rises on merit, and on promoting the best of the best. Such considerations are not—and should not be—limited by gender, race, or identity. Organizations such as Racing Pride work actively with many F1 teams in order to also provide the most welcoming platform for the LGBTQ+ community, both as a fan base and within the factory.

These are just a few examples as all teams are now actively engaged in ensuring a push toward promoting greater diversity, inclusion, and equity within their organizations.

WOMEN DRIVERS IN FORMULA 1

Motor racing is one of the few sports in the world in which men and women compete together. While in other sports there are specific male and female leagues, motorsport has never seen the need to create a parallel ladder. The challenge has always been for a human and a car to work in harmony and for the driver to ultimately make the difference. Once the helmet goes on, gender should be immaterial. All that has ever mattered is how the racing driver fares against the clock.

Danica Patrick was a race winner in IndyCar, Ellen Lohr won in the DTM, and Michèle Mouton very nearly won the World Rally Championship. In 2023, the all-female Iron Dames Le Mans GTE team of Sarah Bovy, Michelle Gatting, and Rahel Frey won the eight hours of Bahrain WEC race and finished second in the championship, while 2022 Ferrari Challenge champion Doriane Pin won a race en route to second place in just a partial campaign in the 2023 F4 SE Asia Championship, while also being crowned the 2023 WEC revelation of the year. Yet in the entire history of Formula 1, only one woman has scored points, and it has been more than thirty years since a woman has even attempted to qualify for a Grand Prix.

But that doesn't mean that no women have tried to climb the ladder and reach Formula 1 in all that time. At the same time as Susie Wolff made it to Formula 1 as a test and reserve driver in the mid-2010s, a number of female racers joined the GP3 (now known as F3) series. But a lack of funding and failing to land at teams that could consistently compete meant even a driver like Alice Powell—who had won a Formula Renault title—was unable to progress any further.

With opportunities seemingly limited and female racers routinely passed over for sponsorship or top-line seats, the decision was made to create a female-only championship, the W Series, in order to allow women the opportunity to shine. This only solved part of the issue, however, as it became apparent that women racers needed more than opportunity and a showcase. The next generation of female talent needed proper training to give them the tools to compete with their male counterparts.

And so, in 2023, the F1 Academy was launched. This all-female championship features five teams of three cars run by squads currently racing in either Formula 3 or Formula 2. The championship gives the racing drivers more track time to better hone their craft, while also providing support with technical, physical, and mental race preparation. With time, F1 Academy should create a strong path for female racers to move up to F3, F2, and hopefully, F1. The championship is run by Susie Wolff, the last woman to drive in Formula 1 competitively.

SUSTAINABILITY

Formula 1 has long been at the forefront of automotive technology, and the developments made on the racetrack have had positive impacts on everyday roads and global society. With the challenges faced by us all to safeguard the future of our planet, Formula 1 has been keen to use the brilliant minds within the sport to lead the march toward greater sustainability, with a key mission statement to be carbon zero by 2030.

The turbo-hybrid era, which began in 2014, is rarely spoken about as the major step forward it actually was in terms of sustainability. The very first internal combustion engines of the late 1800s were only about 17 percent efficient. Incredibly, over the first 120 years of their existence, the road-going engine only increased its thermal efficiency to 30 percent. Over the twelve months leading to 2014, Formula 1's engine designers increased efficiency to 40 percent, and today that figure is well in advance of 50 percent. There has therefore been a greater advance in efficiency in the last ten years than in the previous 120…thanks to Formula 1. But the sport has always been forward facing, ready to tackle the next challenge, and with that in mind, new engine regulations for greater sustainability are planned for 2026.

However, power unit emissions account for less than 1 percent of Formula 1's carbon footprint. Around 7 percent comes from event operations, 19 percent from team factories and facilities, 28 percent from staffing travel and accommodation, and 45 percent from freight logistics. With that in mind, and as part of Formula 1's drive toward being carbon zero by 2030, every race must qualify as an F1 "sustainable spectacle" by 2025, with key targets to be met in order to achieve such a status. At the 2023 Austrian Grand Prix, Formula 1 made first use of its own on-site energy station, powering the paddock, pitlane, and broadcast facilities using only solar power and biofuel.

Team offices, facilities, and factories must become 100 percent renewably powered by 2030, with credible carbon offsets to balance to zero in other areas. In 2023, all ten teams achieved FIA three-star Environmental Accreditation—the highest level of environmental sustainability recognition from the sport's governing body.

Work is continuing to streamline the race calendar, while transportation is being aided with the use of more-efficient planes and flexible shipping containers for fuel-efficient transport. In 2023, Mercedes became the first team to run the fleet of trucks required for European freight transportation on biofuel, delivering an immediate 89 percent reduction in emissions. Formula 1's logistics partner DHL followed suit that same season, drastically cutting the environmental impact of freight transportation.

FUTURE TECHNOLOGY

Formula 1 is due to undergo a major regulation change in 2026: both chassis and engine rules are set to be shaken up as the sport aims to achieve carbon neutrality, while maintaining its pledge to ensure closer racing and better on-track action. The new second-generation power units used in 2026 will be run on fully sustainable "drop-in" fuels. No newly sourced carbon will be burned as Formula 1 fuel suppliers will source fuel from non-food biomass, municipal waste, and the atmosphere itself. This alone should result in a 65 percent reduction in greenhouse gas emissions compared to fossil fuels, and while burning this new fuel will still generate carbon emissions, those emissions will be cyclical, replacing that in the atmosphere which was taken to create it.

The MGU-K used on these new power units will provide three times the electrical power of their current iteration, collecting up to 350 kW under braking as compared to the 120 kW of the current generation. With more power coming from harnessed and reused energy, the use of the new sustainable fuel will be lessened, with 70 kg (154 lbs) set as the target for a Grand Prix distance, down from 100 kg (220 lbs) in 2023. The MGU-H will become a thing of the past to eliminate an element of cost and complexity.

The new engine regulations have seen huge interest from within and outside the sport, with Ferrari, Mercedes, and Alpine (Renault) committing early to these second-generation power units. Both Ford and Honda have declared their return, and Audi has announced its arrival in the sport in 2026, while others have expressed an interest in joining them.

The cars themselves will also undergo a transformation. At nearly 800 kg (1,764 lbs), modern F1 cars are the largest and heaviest in history, and despite their astonishing speed, they are nowhere near as nimble as their predecessors. The plans for 2026 are to reduce the car's dimensions, making them shorter, narrower, and, as a result, lighter. Another element in shrinking the cars will be to reduce the drag inherent in the larger cars' characteristics, ensuring that straight-line speed and overtaking remain key considerations. The lessons learned from the early years of the new aerodynamic regulations imposed in 2022 will form key understandings in the final formulation of the aero regulations for 2026.

The standardization of certain parts is considered a key element of a continuing move to cut costs for all, while the goal of protecting the environment means a likely heightened use of sustainable and recycled materials. All of this, however, comes with safety remaining the key consideration as the sport looks toward active and connected safety systems to ensure that drivers remain as well protected as possible.

F1 AT THE MOVIES

From Formula 1's earliest years, the excitement of the races and the daring of the world's greatest drivers have proved a fertile ground for master storytellers and filmmakers. And while there have been countless documentaries made about the sport dating back to the 1950s, Hollywood studios have also sought to immortalize Formula 1 on the silver screen.

One of the earliest examples was Roger Corman's 1963 movie *The Young Racers*, starring Mark Damon and William Campbell. Despite a relatively limited budget of under $100,000, the filmmakers embedded themselves with Formula 1 for a number of races during the 1962 season, and the movie features some marvelous footage from the time.

With Formula 1 gaining international appeal throughout the 1960s, the big studios came calling. In 1965, John Frankenheimer started researching for his 1966 movie *Grand Prix*, and movie legend Steve McQueen began work on his F1 film *Day of the Champion*. McQueen's hopes of making the first big-budget F1 movie fell through, however, as delays saw Warner Bros. pull the plug on the project. And so it was Frankenheimer, along with stars James Garner and Eva Marie Saint, who had the full 1966 season to themselves to create their opus. Operating on a budget of around $9 million, and taking well over twice that at the box office, *Grand Prix* is still widely regarded as the best F1 movie ever made, winning three Academy Awards in 1967.

Two years later, in 1969, actor Paul Newman completed his American racing movie, *Winning*, and in 1971, McQueen finally finished his own motorsport epic, *Le Mans*, creating what became seen as an unofficial trilogy of motorsport movies covering F1, IndyCar, and sportscars.

Formula 1 next took a starring role in the 1977 movie *Bobby Deerfield*, with Al Pacino cast as the titular character. Brabham boss Bernie Ecclestone agreed to allow filmmakers into the heart of his Grand Prix team, with race footage a vital part of the movie's plotline and various scenes filmed at Brabham's own F1 factory.

It would take another forty years for Formula 1 to feature as the main subject of a Hollywood movie, as broadcast rights tightened and became more exclusive and expensive. Sylvester Stallone came close to making an F1 movie during the 1990s, spending many months in the F1 paddock and working with the sport's bosses on a script. Unhappy with the direction the movie was taking, however, F1 cut ties with the *Rocky* star, and he took his concept to IndyCar, creating what became the critically derided 2001 movie *Driven*.

In the mid-2000s, Pixar's animated *Cars* franchise used the voices of Formula 1 drivers, both legends and heroes of the day, with Mario Andretti, Michael Schumacher, Niki Lauda, Sir Lewis Hamilton, Sebastian Vettel, and numerous others featuring prominently in the movies.

In 2013, Ron Howard released the first major F1 movie since *Bobby Deerfield*, except this time it was based on real events. *Rush* focused on the 1976 Formula 1 season and the championship battle between Niki Lauda and James Hunt. The movie won a BAFTA award, and it brought critical acclaim to both Chris Hemsworth as Hunt and in particular Daniel Brühl for his portrayal of Lauda. Six years later, in 2019, there was an unexpected cameo for the sport in the Adam Sandler and Jennifer Aniston comedy *Murder Mystery*, which involved the movie filming at the Monaco Grand Prix with McLaren and Fernando Alonso.

All of which brings us to the 2020s and a renewed interest from Hollywood to feature Formula 1. Michael Mann's film about the life of Enzo Ferrari, entitled *Ferrari*, was released in 2023, the same year that filming began for the most ambitious F1 movie since *Grand Prix*. Embedding themselves in the sport and traveling to races—as Frankenheimer had done sixty years before—Joseph Kosinski and Jerry Bruckheimer swept from the success of *Top Gun: Maverick* to filming a movie about Formula 1, with Brad Pitt and Damson Idris cast as F1 drivers competing against the field of twenty real-life racing stars.

ACKNOWLEDGMENTS

I'm indebted to the fantastic team at Ten Speed Press and Penguin Random House for approaching me with an offer to work together, and for then having such belief in the concept we created. First and foremost, thank you to Aaron Wehner for your faith in me from the outset, and to the incredible team behind the project, especially Kaitlin Ketchum, Lizzie Allen, Kelly Booth, Kausaur Fahimuddin, Jane Chinn, Joyce Wong, Brianne Sperber, and Jana Branson.

My thanks to Davi Augusto, our amazing illustrator, who is represented by Colagene Paris, without whom we would not have a book. I'm astounded by your artistry and so thankful we got to work together. Tremendous thanks also to Craig Scarborough for your help and time in ensuring the technical drawings were on point.

My family and friends, my incredible wife, and my awe-inspiring daughters: thank you for your love and support.

Thanks to Ben Gorman, my agent, for having my back, making the deals, and kicking my ass.

This book stands on the shoulders of a lifetime of accrued knowledge. For more than thirty years I have read and absorbed the great journals of motor racing and learned from the best writers in the industry, whose understanding and knowledge have formed the backbone of my own. *Autosport, Motorsport News* (or *Motoring News* as it was in my youth), *MotorSport Magazine, F1 Racing, AutoCar, Racer, Autocourse,* and in recent years the online presence of Autosport and Motorsport.com, The Race, and F1.com have been my companions and guides. In particular I am, and the pages of this book are, indebted to the Grand Prix race reporting and feature writing of Gerald Donaldson, David Tremayne, Maurice Hamilton, Alan Henry, Richard Williams, Mark Hughes, Simon Arron, Nigel Roebuck, Joe Saward, James Allen, Edd Straw, and Denis Jenkinson. I must single out David Tremayne for unique thanks: as my first employer, he would test me each and every morning of my young career on the history of the sport and taught me the importance of maintaining that knowledge while working within the evolving modern story of Formula 1.

For statistics and dates, FORIX.com and Wikipedia have been tremendously useful in filling in the gaps and gray areas.

I'm also grateful in the extreme to Formula 1 itself: to Stefano Domenicali for writing such a fantastic foreword; to Liam Parker for his help, friendship, and counsel; to Ian Holmes, David Hill, Dean Locke, Hayley McDaid, Tim Bampton, and all those who have helped and supported me and the project within the wider F1 family. Unending thanks must also go to all the teams in the sport and their PR departments, in particular Adrian Atkinson and Steve Cooper at Aston Martin F1 Aramco Formula 1 Team, to Rebecca Banks at Williams Racing, Thomas Hoffmann (formerly) of Scuderia Ferrari, and Alice Hedworth at Oracle Red Bull Racing. Thanks also to the FIA, especially Tom Wood.

I am also beyond appreciative for the vision of Sean Bratches, Paul Martin, James Gay Rees, and Nat Grouille, which resulted in the phenomenon known as *Drive to Survive*. Being asked to play a small role in this incredible series has been the greatest honor and has unquestionably led to amazing new opportunities, such as writing this book and sharing my love of Formula 1 with a new audience.

And finally, my deepest gratitude to you for reading. This book only scratches the surface of the amazing history of this sport and the incredible characters that have created its exhilarating story. I hope this leads you on a path of further discovery into the more than one thousand races in Formula 1's past, and the many hundreds of drivers and teams who represent the building blocks on which this great sport was created.

ABOUT THE AUTHOR

WILL BUXTON has been actively involved in the highest levels of international motor racing for over two decades. His career started at the turn of the millennium in print journalism, before a three-year stint running the communications department for the GP2 Series. His return to journalism coincided with an opportunity to try his hand at commentary, from where an offer arose to become the F1 pit reporter for the United States.

After a decade on American television, he joined Formula 1's in-house broadcast team as their new push into the digital domain was launched under Liberty Media. Known today around the world for his work on F1 TV and the global Netflix sensation *Formula 1: Drive to Survive,* he is one of the most recognized and respected voices in the sport, and in 2023 reported on his 600th motor race and attended his 300th Grand Prix.

INDEX

Published in the United States by Ten Speed Press, an imprint of the Crown
Publishing Group, a division of Penguin Random House LLC, New York.
TenSpeed.com

Ten Speed Press and the Ten Speed Press colophon are registered
trademarks of Penguin Random House LLC.

Illustrations on 21, 22, and 23 by Craig Scarborough

Typefaces: Joshua Darden's Freight Sans and Contrast Foundry's CoFo Kak

Library of Congress Cataloging-in-Publication Data
Names: Buxton, Will, author.
Title: Grand Prix : an illustrated history of Formula 1 / Will Buxton.
Description: First edition. | California : Ten Speed Press, [2024] | Includes
    index. Identifiers: LCCN 2023040852 (print) | LCCN 2023040853 (ebook) |
    ISBN 9781984863249 (hardcover) | ISBN 9781984863256 (ebook)
Subjects: LCSH: Grand Prix racing—History—Pictorial works. | FIA Formula
    One World Championship—History—Pictorial works. | Formula One
    automobiles—History—Pictorial works.
Classification: LCC GV1029.15 .B88 2024 (print) | LCC GV1029.15 (ebook) |
    DDC 796.7209—dc23/eng/20230902
LC record available at https://lccn.loc.gov/2023040852
LC ebook record available at https://lccn.loc.gov/2023040853

Hardcover ISBN: 978-1-9848-6324-9
eBook ISBN: 978-1-9848-6325-6

Printed in China

Acquiring editor: Aaron Wehner | Editor: Kaitlin Ketchum
Production editor: Joyce Wong | Editorial assistant: Kausaur Fahimuddin
Designer and art director: Lizzie Allen
Production designers: Mari Gill and Faith Hague
Production manager: Jane Chinn
Copyeditor: Jeff Campbell | Proofreader: Janet Renard | Indexer: Jay Kreider
Marketer: Brianne Sperber | Publicist: Jana Branson

10 9 8 7 6 5 4 3 2 1

First Edition